MAN, BEAST AND VIRTUE

First published in 1989 by Absolute Classics, an imprint of
Absolute Press, 14 Widcombe Crescent, Bath, England

© Charles Wood 1989

Series Editor: Giles Croft

Cover and text design: Ian Middleton

Printed by WBC Print, Bristol
Bound by W. H. Ware & Son, Clevedon

ISBN 0 948230 24 X

MAN, BEAST AND VIRTUE

Luigi Pirandello

A new version by Charles Wood

absolute classics

INTRODUCTION

Disorientation and disgust greeted the first production of Pirandello's
MAN, BEAST AND VIRTUE in Milan in 1919 for its comic
depiction of adultery, marital obligation, and the frantic efforts of a
terrified lover to ensure that the "right thing" be done. Pirandello
talked of theatre being the art of the broom in which a dramatist
wields a brush rather than a pen, broad sweeps of paint rather than
delicate washes of colour, large gestures and instantly understood
ideas. When he came to write his own plays, his ideas found
expression in a form which had also swept away the fashionable,
florid, over-written literary drama of the Italian stage in the early
1900's. The broom of the dramatist used in a more mundane sense.

MAN, BEAST AND VIRTUE is a comedy full of dark irony. The
central character, Paolino, believes himself to be a man of honour and
learning, a true man of science, a hater of lies and dissembling. He
finds himself forced by circumstances to indulge in the very vices he
despises and abhors in others. It is also a comedy in the strictest sense
in that it explores the weaknesses and contradictions of human
behaviour. In this it has its origins, as all true comedy has, in the
comedies of the Greek theatre which were about man and his search
for his own consciousness of being; the struggle to disentangle himself
from the arms, the promptings, the commands and the compulsions of
the "Gods".

CHARLES WOOD

MAN, BEAST AND VIRTUE received its British première in this version at the National Theatre in 1989. The cast was as follows:

TOTO (A pharmacist)	William Hoyland
ROSARIA (Paolino's housekeeper)	Brid Brennan
PAOLINO (A private tutor)	Trevor Eve
GIGLIO (His pupils) BELLI	Neil Clark Sean Gascoine
MRS. PERELLA	Marion Bailey
NONO (Her son)	Mark Goodwin/Todd Welling
DR PULEJO (A physician)	Tom Chadbon
GRAZIA (The Perellas' maid)	Pauline Delany
FILIPPO (A sailor)	Anthony Douse
CAPTAIN PERELLA	Terence Rigby

DIRECTOR	William Gaskill
DESIGNER	Annie Smart
LIGHTING	Mick Hughes
MUSIC ASSISTANT	John White

ACT ONE

Seagulls. The sound of ships. Leaving and entering harbour.

Scene: the house of Paolino in Leghorn 1919.

> *A modest house with comfortable overstuffed furniture
> of a mixture of styles and ages and states of repair and
> thousands of books, on shelves some of them, piled
> others of them; on chairs and on the floor.
> Doors leading to cupboards, one of them very large and
> full of books.
> Discovered, the room in more than usual disorder,
> chairs upended, tables in the centre, sofa and arm
> chairs out of place.
> The study is being cleaned.*
>
> *The voice of Toto heard off.*

TOTO: It doesn't matter.

ROSARIA: Why do you do it, sir?

> *Enter Rosaria.*

Every morning, first thing, before I've had time to get things straight, you do it.

> *Enter Toto.*

TOTO: Does it matter, Rosaria?

> *Rosaria is housekeeper to Paolino; she clucks like a
> hen, hair inexpertly dyed red, scarf and curling papers.
> Toto wears his hat, moves neatly, is a hand washer,
> just below chin level; a contrite fox, sanctimonious as a
> priest he is nevertheless a pharmacist.*

ROSARIA: Of course it matters, sir.

TOTO: It doesn't matter to me, and I have to give you the key.

ROSARIA: Might I suggest you give me the key at the door, then there is no need for you to come in, find things like this.

TOTO: I like coming in. You're not being very pleasant to me this morning, Rosaria.

ROSARIA: You must see that I'm busy, sir. I have a great deal to
            do and there you stand, forgive me, with me still . . .
            like I am.

TOTO: It's simply because of my brother, poor chap, his
            vigilance all night at the hospital Rosaria, poor fellow
            . . . Like what?

ROSARIA: Oh please, I have nothing against your worthy brother
            the doctor, you know I'll give him the key . . . My hair
            still in curlers.

TOTO: Oh Rosaria, that is really of no importance.

ROSARIA: And my chairs exposed.

TOTO: I beg your pardon?

ROSARIA: Forgive me but a respectable house has its modesty.
            Like a respectable woman it should not be seen . . . should
            not be seen not tidy.

TOTO: I respect that and I love to hear you say it, Rosaria.

ROSARIA: Oh do you, sir?

TOTO: I do wholeheartedly, and I agree with you, I believe
            that what you say is true.

ROSARIA: But please sir, oh please sir don't take offence but you
            come in like a Hun!

TOTO: Oh no!

ROSARIA: Forgive me but you rape it.

TOTO: I do not.

ROSARIA: I have to say it, you violate its modesty.

            Toto, hand on the leg of a chair.

TOTO: I?

ROSARIA: Yes, I have to say it, you sir!

            *Toto jerks nervously away as she interposes herself
            between him and the exposed legs of her chairs.*

            You violate the modesty of this house, no matter how I
            struggle to preserve it, struggle . . . who . . .

> *Rosaria setting the chairs on their feet, tugging down the loose covers, like skirts around their wooden ankles.*

Who would be a chair in this house?

TOTO: Who?

ROSARIA: Forgive me but what with you . . .

> *Now having worked herself up into a rage, glaring at him, beyond him.*

. . . peering, every morning, leering at my chairs before they're fit to be seen, I'm sorry but I have to say it, and him!

> *Glaring so hard at the door beyond Toto and with such rage that Toto flinches.*

Him! He can't keep his hands off of them neither. What he does to them is abuse! Ranting and raving and his great hands up their backs; the brute, shoving them, shaking them, in the air waving them . . . across the floor, kicking them, throwing them . . .

TOTO: Rosaria, you dote on them, as if they were your children.

ROSARIA: I become attached to things. I do dote. I want to keep them precious and intact and gleaming and shy, as a new bride is.

TOTO: Ah, a home!

ROSARIA: You have a home sir, over the road.

TOTO: When I say home, my dear Rosaria, I mean a home home, a family . . .

ROSARIA: Perhaps you ought to find yourself a wife then, sir . . .

TOTO: Oh no!

> *Toto horrified at the thought.*

ROSARIA: Or you could employ a housekeeper who might become fond of you, which would be a very good thing for your brother the worthy doctor, it would be something for him. You ought to marry, sir.

TOTO: I don't think so. Not I. Not married. My brother the

    doctor, he could and I would be very happy to see it
    happen, that I mean, sincerely. But he won't marry,
    because he need not, because I am there.

ROSARIA: Can you give him everything a wife might?

TOTO: Yes. No! However, he doesn't feel the need for a wife.
    I do everything, I see to everything . . . You know that,
    you know me. It's all done, all spick and span for him,
    it's my pleasure. That house is for my brother, not for
    me.

ROSARIA: That's because you're out all day.

TOTO: He's out all day, poor devoted wretch. He's on duty all
    night, at bedsides all day. He has his house calls. I have
    the pharmacy. But it isn't home you know. Not for him
    or for me. Home is never the home we make for
    ourselves, Rosaria, put together, tend with care . . .
    what we mean by home, what we taste when we savour
    the word in our memory, bitter sweet, is the home
    made for us by others, mother and father, their caring,
    their thought. But they too thought of another home,
    that made for them by their parents. And that's that.
    How it always is.

    Enter Paolino in a rush.

    Paolino. Here he is. We talk of homes.

PAOLINO: Do you though?

    Paolino is thirtyish, full of feverish impatient life,
    every emotion obvious, every reaction of his soul.
    He won't be answered back, he will not listen, is given
    to abrupt changes of mood, tone, temper.

    Give him his coffee and get shut of him, Rosaria.

TOTO: I don't come here for coffee.

PAOLINO: Don't be a hypocrite as well as mean, Toto. Have your
    coffee and piss off.

TOTO: Oh no . . . I was just chatting.

PAOLINO: About home.

TOTO: That's right.

PAOLINO: I heard it, on and on and on, the rhapsody of home.

TOTO: Heartfelt, Paolino.

PAOLINO: Absolutely. Because you're tight-fisted; give him his coffee. It's an excuse, to cover your meanness, Toto.

TOTO: That's awful! If that's what you think, I'll go.

PAOLINO: No you won't!

TOTO: It isn't true. I would rather go.

PAOLINO: You'll drink your bloody coffee. And it is true. You are mean.

TOTO: No, no . . .

PAOLINO: And because it is true, and you are mean you'll have your coffee if I have to pour it down your throat.

TOTO: I don't want it.

PAOLINO: I don't care what you want, you'll have it. Not one cup of coffee, but two, three, four!

TOTO: No.

PAOLINO: You've earned them. Yes, earned them. I feel much better now. I have let off steam. That's grand, got it off my chest, put you in your place, I have relieved myself of my . . . my steam. You can have a daily cup of coffee. Rosaria, he can count on it. Now, out! Go on.

Shoving Toto out, Toto stopping at the door.

Not a word. I don't need thanks.

TOTO: I wasn't going to. I'd rather you let me . . .

PAOLINO: Pay? Eh?

TOTO: At the end of the month.

PAOLINO: Am I a café? Do I sell coffee?

TOTO: No, no but . . . the thing is, in my house I have nobody to make me coffee, you have, you've got your housekeeper . . . you don't make coffee just to sell it to me, you make it for yourself don't you, anyway? What you do now is one extra cup, you let off steam, and I pay you for it. How much?

PAOLINO: Toto, suppose I find myself a wife.

TOTO: You do?

PAOLINO: Yes. Suppose. I go out and get one for myself. Not for you, not to sell to you, no . . . for me but, suppose I let you have a bit of her, five minutes or so, just a cup or so, say every day, five minutes a day or so, just a cup, just a slice of her?

TOTO: I'm not talking about your wife.

PAOLINO: I don't have a wife.

TOTO: I'm not . . .

PAOLINO: I do have a housekeeper.

ROSARIA: That's right.

TOTO: I'm not . . .

PAOLINO: Coffee . . .

TOTO: . . . talking about Rosaria.

PAOLINO: . . . does not happen.

ROSARIA: It doesn't.

PAOLINO: It doesn't make itself. Idiot! It is made for a professor by a housekeeper, fact of life. The reason why professors keep housekeepers is coffee.

ROSARIA: And things like that.

PAOLINO: Labourers don't need to keep housekeepers because they are able to make their own coffee, which is why labourers are so much better off than we professors. Labourers are very lucky people, they can do everything for themselves without loss of dignity and . . . they know how to. Professors don't, can't, a professor is forced . . . obliged to have a housekeeper.

ROSARIA: To do for him. Her uttermost, smooth his bed for him, plump his cushions with scarce a thought for herself, his every comfort her only . . .

PAOLINO: Thank you, enough.

ROSARIA: That's as may be . . . without me you'd be odd socks, threads, unravelled, unshaven, unkempt . . .

PAOLINO: Thank you.

ROSARIA: Shirt cuffs, not knowing what cloud he's on, he's
            absent-minded, very, and scruffy, very . . .

PAOLINO: You!

TOTO: Me?

PAOLINO: You brought that on. Why should I alone have to
            suffer all that, just because I'm a professor, just
            because I teach, just because I have the good fortune to
            be a man of standing and learning who can't boil an
            egg, while you, pharmacist, get off scot-free? You feel
            like telling someone, Rosaria, tell him.

ROSARIA: I would. Only I don't do for him.

PAOLINO: Precisely!

                Shoving Toto.

            Out. From tomorrow no bloody coffee, not one drop.

TOTO: That's a bit much . . .

PAOLINO: Toto, go to hell!

TOTO: . . . and you called me an idiot. I've a very good degree
            in pharmaceutical science.

PAOLINO: Idiot! Tell you what, every time I call you an idiot you
            can claim a cup of coffee. So that's tomorrow's cup.
            Want some more? It's a cup of coffee per insult. More?

TOTO: No thank you.

                Exit Toto hurriedly.
                Exit Rosaria with:

ROSARIA: That'll teach you to keep your sticky hands off of my
            chair legs . . .

                Paolino composes himself, deep breathing.
                He groans:

PAOLINO: God, what people!

                The bleat of a goat off.
                Paolino groans again.

            Ohhhhhhhhh!

The chatter of a chimpanzee.

Ohhhhhhhhh Christ! Here starteth the first lesson.

Paolino puts his face in his hands.

Yes.

Enter Giglio and Belli.
They are two boys or lads or young men, pupils. Giglio is like a goat with wild black hair, his voice the bleat from his gangly frame.
Belli is an ape wearing spectacles, his laugh the chatter of a chimpanzee from his knuckles-to-the-floor frame.
Their reassuringly animal-like appearances are wrapped in scarves, one red, one blue.
Textbooks encumber them, drop from them, spin from their toes and are gathered up and strapped to fall again.
They utter with a bleat and a chatter:

GIGLIO: May I come in, sir?

BELLI: Sir, may I come in, sir?

            Paolino, face in hands, shudders, waits for bleat and chatter to die, then sighing, says:

PAOLINO: Come in.

GIGLIO: Good morning, sir.

BELLI: Good morning, sir.

            Paolino galvanises himself into a flurry of movement and mimicry as the boys go to their desks and he to his chair, slouching forward in imitation of them both.

PAOLINO: Good morning, sir.

GIGLIO: May I sit down, sir?

BELLI: May I sit down, sir?

PAOLINO: Sit down. May I sit down?

GIGLIO: Thank you, sir.

BELLI: Thank you, sir.

PAOLINO: Thank you, Giglio. Thank you, Belli. Don't mention it, Giglio; don't you, dear Belli . . . ooooooooooooh!

Glaring at them from his chair, shaking his head at their smiles, he splutters in exasperation:

Good God! Good God!

GIGLIO: Sir?

BELLI: Sir?

PAOLINO: God! I firmly believe life among men will soon become impossible for me.

GIGLIO: Why, sir?

BELLI: Do you mean because of us, sir?

Paolino stands, screwing himself up. His hands holding his chair in front of him, strangling it.
Then he quickly tucks the seat under him, sits, looking at his pupils from over the chair's back, asking quietly in spite of his suppressed rage:

PAOLINO: How old are we? You? You?

GIGLIO: Eighteen, sir.

BELLI: Seventeen, sir.

PAOLINO: Yes, we are . . .

Shaking his head at the enormity of what he is about to say:

. . . men. Hair grows apace, chin, lip, crotch. Doesn't it? Both men, now.

Bleat, chatter, itch of hair, scratch of bewilderment.

What . . . is the Greek for actor don't look at your vocabularies . . . you?

GIGLIO: Me, sir?

PAOLINO: Did I say, me sir?

GIGLIO: The Greek?

PAOLINO: Did I say Persian?

Paolino leaves the struggling Giglio.

You don't know. You?

BELLI: Me, sir? For actor, sir? It's slipped . . .

PAOLINO: Whoops!

Paolino grasping for a slipping jellyfish of a thought.

BELLI: . . . my mind, sir, actor.

PAOLINO: Whoops, slipped your mind has it? You mean you did
             know once, but, whoops, slipped, doesn't come to mind
             now?

BELLI: Oh no, sir. I have never recalled knowing it.

PAOLINO: Ah! Well, what you should say is; I – do – not – know!
             I – do – not – know! Not, whoops slipped my . . . I
             will tell you what it is. The Greek for actor is
             upocritès There. Why? Why upocritès? What do
             actors do?

BELLI: They act, sir, I think . . .

PAOLINO: Not sure?

BELLI: They do, I think.

PAOLINO: You think. Do you think it's fair to call an actor doing
             his job, you think, acting; a hypocrite? Doing his job,
             pursuing his profession. You can't call him a hypocrite
             for that. Who *can* you call hypocrite then, this word the
             Greeks gave their actors? You.

Pointing at Giglio.

GIGLIO: I know, sir. Somebody who pretends, sir.

PAOLINO: There! You are right. Just like an actor pretends to be
             a king, an emperor even, when he hasn't got two coins
             to rub together in real life, when he is penniless, in a
             tinsel crown.

GIGLIO: Yaaaaaaaah!

BELLI: Yeahhhhhhhh!

PAOLINO: You jeer. What do you jeer at? An actor does his job,
             there's nothing wrong with an actor doing his job.
             When is it wrong? I'll tell you, when it's malicious,
             when it's habit, when one is not an actor but a person
             going about the business of life; when it is to one's
             smiling advantage to pretend. Out of politeness,
             because being polite is to pretend; and how we do it,

our souls black as night, as the feathers of a crow inside
but outside white as those of a dove; inside one's throat
the bitterness of gall, on one's lips the sweetness of
honey; and such as; "Good morning, sir" instead of;
"Go to hell, sir!", eh?

GIGLIO: Oh, sir!

BELLI: I say!

PAOLINO: What?

GIGLIO: Go to hell, sir?

BELLI: Is that what we should say, sir? I say.

PAOLINO: I would prefer it. I would. Truly, I would, or . . . for
            God's sake, just say nothing.

GIGLIO: And then . . .

PAOLINO: What?

GIGLIO: You'd say we were bad mannered.

BELLI: What a bad mannered pair!

PAOLINO: I would. Quite right. Because being polite insists that
            we wish good morning to somebody we would willingly
            consign to hell. Being polite means being a hypocrite.
            Quod erat demonstrandum! Now, history.

BELLI: I don't . . .

GIGLIO: But, sir . . .

PAOLINO: Enough! Over, enough said, politeness is ruining my
            digestion. History.

            *A knock on the door, Rosaria comes round the doorway
            and gestures.*

            We'll start with you, Belli . . . what's that? Who's that?

ROSARIA: Me, sir, come over here, sir.

PAOLINO: When I'm giving a lesson . . .

ROSARIA: A moment, sir.

PAOLINO: You know very well that when a lesson is in
            progress . . .

ROSARIA: I know that, blessed Mary and Joseph and the little
           ones, I know that, suffer little children . . . that's why,
           that's why, if you don't mind me saying so, that's why
           it must be urgent mustn't it?

PAOLINO: Excuse me, gentlemen, for a moment.

           Going to Rosaria.

           What is so urgent?

ROSARIA: There's a lady says she's a close friend. You are a close
           friend of hers. With a boy.

PAOLINO: One of my pupils? A mother?

ROSARIA: That is as may be. She's in a great taking . . .

PAOLINO: Taking?

ROSARIA: She's taking on so. When she asked could she see you
           she went white as a sheet, then red as lead . . . blushing
           every colour . . .

PAOLINO: Who is she?

ROSARIA: A close friend. You are, of her. Red as lead. White
           as . . .

PAOLINO: Her name?

ROSARIA: Her name?

PAOLINO: How many times have I told you, ask them their
           name . . .

ROSARIA: I did. Mrs. . . . Mrs. Per . . .

PAOLINO: Sssshhhhh! Mrs. Perella?

ROSARIA: Mrs. Pe . . .

PAOLINO: Sssssshhhh! Here? Oh God, what's happened? Er . . .
           wait . . . er . . .

ROSARIA: She said she was a friend.

PAOLINO: Ask her to wait . . . yes, wait a few minutes.

ROSARIA: So you do know her!

PAOLINO: Never you mind. Tell her to wait, that's right, wait.

ROSARIA: She said you did.

Exit Rosaria.
Close friend.

PAOLINO: Yes, yes, yes . . . so.
           Back to his pupils, pulling himself together.
           So, where were we? Boys, let's not . . . er . . . Er . . .
           lose time.

BELLI: History, sir.

PAOLINO: No no, instead of that, instead of history and geography
           you can do me another little translation.

GIGLIO: Oh no, sir.

BELLI: Oh no, sir.

PAOLINO: From Italian into Latin.

GIGLIO: No sir, please sir.

BELLI: No sir, please sir.

           They both quickly sit on their Latin dictionaries.

GIGLIO: We did it yesterday.

BELLI: It's always Latin, always Latin.

PAOLINO: It's your weakest subject.

GIGLIO: We're fed up with Latin.

PAOLINO: Enough! Enough . . . you can translate . . . you can . . .
           Searching for a book through a pile, on his knees.

GIGLIO: We've lost our dictionaries.

BELLI: Me as well, lost it.

           *Paolino grabs two dictionaries and tosses them at the
           boys, then finds the book he is looking for, still on his
           knees.*

           Dictionaries. Two more.

GIGLIO: But sir . . .

PAOLINO: Enough! No more, you'll translate this . . . yes . . .

           *Reluctantly the boys approach and peer over the
           shoulders of the distracted teacher, still on his knees.
           Paolino looks up from the book.*

That she should come at this time.

Then down again at the book, muttering to himself.

What time of the morning is this for her to appear?

He then becomes aware of the two boys at his shoulder.

What do you want?

GIGLIO: The translation.

BELLI: You're reading.

PAOLINO: Eh? Yes, that's right, this, translate this short passage, yes . . . illud maxim rerum est eorum . . . yes.

GIGLIO: Oh dear.

Paolino shoves them the book and springs to his feet, opening the door of the cupboard, books tumble from it.

PAOLINO: In here, both of you!

Belli and Giglio aghast.

BELLI: In there?

PAOLINO: You'll love it in there, a den, that's what it is, lovely and warm, lots of books, lots of dictionaries, lots of cribs . . . In you go. Lovely little room.

GIGLIO: It's a cupboard.

PAOLINO: No no, plenty of room. It's a little room . . . come on!

He pushes them in.

BELLI: But sir, we can't see a thing.

PAOLINO: Of course you can, but . . . no copying mind, no looking over each other's shoulder, I want it to be your own unaided work. I shall know if you copy! In! To work, to work . . . soon finish it and then you can come out . . . In!

Closing the door on the struggling boys and tumbling books.

In you little buggers.

Enter Mrs. Perella with Nono, her son.
Paolino with his back to the cupboard door.

Come in, madam, do come in.

Mrs. Perella is virtue personified.
She is the most perfect blend of modesty, virtue and
prudishness, she is also unfortunately two months
pregnant by Paolino and she can't stop being sick.
Or wanting to be sick, or thinking she is about to be
sick.
She has come to tell her lover Paolino that her fears
have been confirmed but because of Nono she can't say
anything openly, and because of her crippling modesty,
and because of her sickness, or her fears of sickness
every time she opens her mouth she fears she is going to
be sick; so whatever she has to say she says through a
handkerchief demurely wielded as if dabbing away
tears.
Mrs. Perella is deeply distressed that in spite of her
modesty, her virtue and her prudishness, fate has dealt
her the blow of pregnancy. She keeps her eyes lowered
except for fleeting glances of anguish when Nono
cannot possibly see.
Her clothes sit awkwardly, fashion has a habit of
making virtue look ridiculous. But Mrs. Perella must
wear what fashion decrees no matter how much it
distresses her to be forced to do so.
She speaks in a strange querulous voice, a voice not
hers, a voice from a mouth opened and closed by an
invisible puppet master, a clumsy imitation of a sad
woman's voice.

Yes?

Mrs. Perella gags, her handkerchief to her mouth at
once.

Oh God? Yes? Yes . . . oh God.

Mrs. Perella signalling frantically with her eyes at
Nono who smirks at Paolino.
Nono looks like an appealing cat. Like a cat his head
follows every movement Paolino makes, the head
moving on immobile shoulders.
Nono laughs and smirks a lot, and sniffs a lot but
never ever uses the large clean carefully folded
handkerchief in his left hand pocket.

> *Nono wears a magnificent huge red bow tie and a
> starched white collar.*
> *His eyes are bright as buttons when they don't close
> and consider; as a cat might. His whole being begs for
> the pat on the head, the gentle stroke which Paolino
> resists.*

Dear Nono, you're here.

NONO: Good morning.

PAOLINO: Yes. Good good morning, there is a good boy, Nono.
Good morning. Yes.

> *Then galvanised into action he seizes a chair as if its
> last moment has come and places it screaming for Mrs.
> Perella to sit on, asking:*

Not a shadow of a . . . doubt?

> *The frantic eyes of Mrs. Perella towards her son.*

A good morning. Absolutely certain . . . it's a good
morning? So . . .

> *Straight round to Nono asking:*

. . . you've come to see your teacher, my little Nono,
have you?

> *"No no" says Nono, always, with his finger, a habit,
> but with every other part of him as well before he
> answers anything.*

NONO: We've been to the Porto Mediceo, to the harbour.

PAOLINO: Ah yes? To see the ships?

> *No no.*

NONO: To find out what time Papa docks with the *Segesta*.
There's mother opening her mouth again!

> *Mrs. Perella is opening her mouth like a fish as she sits
> on the chair provided for her by Paolino; who jerks
> back from Nono to see her gaping.*

PAOLINO: What?

NONO: Like a fish does.

Paolino looking at the open mouth, alarmed.
Asks Nono:

PAOLINO: What's wrong with her mouth?

Then Mrs. Perella:

Your mouth? What's up with it?

Mrs. Perella getting up, waving her arm, lurching
towards the bookshelves, grasping for a shelf, toppling
books, leaning on the shelf, mouth still open, the
handkerchief to it, wildly signalling to Paolino to leave
her, concentrate on Nono.
The strange voice:

MRS.
PERELLA: Please, for God's sake, him . . . him. Please don't
trouble. Please don't trouble!

Nono nodding his head.

NONO: She's been doing that, mouth open mouth open, for
three days.

PAOLINO: Oh, really?

NONO: Like a fish on a slab.

PAOLINO: Oh no, oh no, she's yawning that's all. I expect she's
tired. Your mother's yawning . . .

NONO: For three days.

PAOLINO: Very tired . . . Mothers get tired . . .

Nono saying no no, his finger wagging, then pointing to
his stomach.

. . . of all sorts of . . .

NONO: It's something down here. I know.

PAOLINO: What?

MRS.
PERELLA: Whaaaaaaaa!

PAOLINO: What are you saying, dear . . . boy?

NONO: It's her tummy. She said so.

PAOLINO: She did?

NONO: A tummy upset, she said.

PAOLINO: Of course, wonderful, something she ate, how dreadful,
           a tummy upset, oh dear, just a little tummy bug . . . er
           . . . upset, that's all dear dear little Nono.

MRS.
PERELLA: Oh! God!

NONO: She spits it up into her hanky, look, ever such a lot
           comes up, look!

PAOLINO: What a thing to say, Nono!

MRS.
PERELLA: Oh dear . . .

PAOLINO: You shouldn't say such things, Nono.

NONO: Why not? She is . . . look.

PAOLINO: Really! You shouldn't . . .

MRS.
PERELLA: He does . . . even in front of the maid.

NONO: What's wrong with that?

PAOLINO: Wrong? Nothing wrong, no, but is it good manners to
           discuss your mother's . . . tummy, in front of a
           servant?

           Mrs. Perella in her strange voice.

MRS.
PERELLA: He says things, he says things in front of everyone . . .

           *Then a change of voice, totally natural, which is what
           happens when she is hurt or speaking urgently, the
           strange voice forgotten:*

           His father. He'll come straight out with it. He's
           arriving today, his father.

           *Paolino staggers, thunderstruck. Mrs. Perella clutches
           at the cupboard door, drapes herself on it, against it.*

PAOLINO: Today! His father is home today?

NONO: Great! Today, papa is home today. Can I go on board?
           I want to go on board with the sailor, can I? Please?

Nono hugging his mother hard.

PAOLINO: Don't! Don't crowd her, Nono.

NONO: Don't worry, she's all right now, look! Nothing's coming up.

Nono hugging his mother again, and pleading:

Can I? Can I? It's great, up on the bridge with papa, he's a captain, he wears a captain's hat and an oilskin coat and he gives orders do that do this, coming alongside, do that do this, coming into dock . . . can I? Can I? He sends for me to come aboard. At once. Can I, mama? Can I?

MRS.
PERELLA: Yes, oh yes . . . you can go.

NONO: Great, great . . . vwhooovwhooo! Vwhooovwhooo!

The siren. Then Nono uses his hands as a megaphone to say:

Get your thumbs from your arses and avast heaving you twerps!

Mrs. Perella breathes over his head her fear:

MRS.
PERELLA: I'm terrified of what he'll say.

NONO: Vwhooovwhooo!

Paolino grabs Nono by an arm as he manoeuvres his ship into the dock and swings him round to say:

PAOLINO: That's enough, the noise, can't you see your mother's not well?

Nono can, over Paolino's shoulder, he laughs in delight.

NONO: Look at her mouth! Look, she's opening it again . . . op op op op! She looks like a fish. I said she did, it's very funny the way she looks like a fish, op op!

PAOLINO: What a perfect little . . . son you are. What a fine young fellow altogether. Your mother is feeling thoroughly wretched and you . . . make the best of it, have a good laugh. What a good boy! Bet you can't

wait to tell your papa so he can have a good laugh as
well, eh? So you can both watch with delight your
mother opening her mouth like a fish. What larks! First
thing you'll tell him. What a happy family reunion it
will be. What a good little chap you are, aren't you
dear little Nono?

*Paolino lifts a beautifully decorated and illustrated
volume from his desk, still in tissue which he removes,
a new book with mouth watering colours and drawings.*

I was going to give you this book . . .

NONO: Ooooooh!

PAOLINO: Which I bought for you yesterday.

NONO: Insects! Great . . . please.

PAOLINO: No no, Nono. You don't get it. You are unkind to your
           mother. So, I shall give it to another of my pupils.

           *A sudden knocking. A bleat and chatter. A scream
           from Mrs. Perella who bounces from the cupboard
           door.*

GIGLIO/
BELLI: Sir! Sir!

MRS.
PERELLA: Oh my God! Who is it?

PAOLINO: It's nothing. Two young beasts, two pupils of mine.
           Hard at work, revising, translating.

NONO: Locked in there? Great, what have they done? Great.

           *Paolino opening the door a chink, keeping his shoulder
           hard up against it to prevent pupils spilling out.*

PAOLINO: What the devil do you want? You can't have finished
           yet.

           Nono peering through his legs into the cupboard.

NONO: What have they done? What have they done? Are they
           incorrigible?

MRS.
PERELLA: Come here, Nono. At once!

GIGLIO: We can't see.

BELLI: We can't read the print in our dictionaries.

GIGLIO: We need a light, and he's got his elbow in my ear.

PAOLINO: All right, be quiet.

Paolino trying to close the door.

A perfectly reasonable request.

Paolino succeeding.

They can't see to read. I'll get them a candle.

Paolino going out.

NONO: Why have you hidden them in there?

PAOLINO: I haven't hidden them, they're doing a translation.

NONO: In the dark?

PAOLINO: No. I'm going to get a candle for them. Perfectly
            reasonable request . . .

Nono goes to pick up the book, Paolino grabs it.

You're not having that! I told you.

Exit Paolino with book. To get the candle.
Giglio and Belli stick their heads out and smile with
great understanding and malice at Mrs. Perella who
gasps in fright and embarrassment.
They also stick their tongues out at Nono who asks
quietly, smiling:

NONO: Why didn't he just flog them?

Re-enter Paolino with a lighted candle.

They stuck their heads out while you were out of the
room, both of them.

Mrs. Perella squeaks.

MRS.
PERELLA: They saw me. They know who I am!

NONO: Stuck their heads out, first one and then the other, and
            they did this to me.

He sticks his tongue out.

They made mama go op op op op!

PAOLINO: I'm sorry. I didn't turn the key.

NONO: Are they completely incorrigible?

Paolino opens the door, and shoves in the candle.

PAOLINO: Here's a candle.

NONO: I'd flog them. Op op op op, she went.

PAOLINO: Get on with your work!

He locks the door, contemplates Nono calmly though he is seething within.

This book. Would you like to have it after all?

NONO: Oh yes.

PAOLINO: Very well, you may have it . . .

NONO: Great . . .

PAOLINO: . . . on condition you never mention your mother's mouth . . .

NONO: It's no good, look, she's doing it again, and I haven't said anything . . . Op op op . . .

Paolino collapses.

PAOLINO: Oh God, this is awful, awful.

Paolino pushes Nono down into a chair and swivels it round so that the boy has his back to his mother, then he places the book in front of Nono on another chair.

If you promise, you can have the book after all, here, but you must promise. If you don't keep your mouth shut, the book goes! Here. Just sit still and look at all the pretty spiders.

Over to Mrs. Perella where he hisses:

This is awful! It couldn't be more obvious what is going on.

MRS.
PERELLA: I am doomed. Finished. Ruined. There is no way forward for me but death.

PAOLINO: What on earth are you saying?

MRS.
PERELLA: I swear it. It is true.

PAOLINO: You must not give up hope. There is hope. There must
            be hope.

MRS.
PERELLA: Don't you realise that should I open my mouth in front
            of my husband I am doomed?

PAOLINO: Well, don't. Keep your bloody mouth shut!

            *Mrs. Perella goes back to her natural voice to say in
            reproof:*

MRS.
PERELLA: I can't help it. It suddenly comes over me.

            Back to her querulous voice:

            Exactly the same thing happened when I was expecting
            Nono. It just comes up.

PAOLINO: Up? You mean your husband has seen it happen, op op
            op?

MRS.
PERELLA: Yes yes, he used to laugh, just as Nono does now.

PAOLINO: Oh God, he'll know at once!

MRS.
PERELLA: The game is up. I am doomed.

PAOLINO: Can't you make an effort not to, can't you control it,
            can't you keep your mouth shut?

MRS.
PERELLA: It comes up from here, my tummy, suddenly. It's a
            sort of contraction.

PAOLINO: Is it?

NONO: Oh look, mummy, this is wonderful! It's a spider,
            spinning his web.

            *Paolino grabs Nono who is on his way to his mother,
            turns him, at first angrily, then carefully and*

exaggeratedly affectionate, shoving him down into the chair, the book propped in front of the boy.

PAOLINO: Isn't that nice! Dear dear dear DEAR little Nono, a spider and his web, how wonderful, you just look at it yourself and there are lots of other charming creatures, lots and lots, you look at them on your own there's a dear little Nono, and mummy will look at them with you later, when she's . . .

Knocking on the cupboard door.

BELLI: Sir! Sir!

PAOLINO: I swear I'll kill them! I will, so help me . . .

A pat on Nono's head which is more of a blow.

When she's better, Nono . . . better.

And Paolino is at the cupboard, opening it a crack and shouting:

What is it now?

Belli sticking his head out over the head of Paolino stuck into the cupboard.

BELLI: Not only, but also, sir.

Paolino pops his head back into view, like a cork from a bottle, dishevelled, slightly disorientated.

PAOLINO: What? But also what?

Belli squeezes out his book, awkwardly above his head so that it looks strange.
He looks up at it.

BELLI: What it says here, sir. Not only, but also, that's the adversative construction is it not, sir?

PAOLINO: How can it be, you ass? I didn't tell you to do that. Adversative? Rubbish! Can't you see that it's expressing co-ordination?

Giglio has his head out at last, his is the hand holding the book.

GIGLIO: I told him that, I told him that, sir. I did. Increasing in intensity and value, sir.

PAOLINO: Even this little twerp, little dear little chap here knows that . . . not only but also, Nono!

Nono straight to his feet, at a position of attention.

NONO: Non Solum!

Paolino slightly taken aback.

PAOLINO: Excellent! Er . . . quite . . . er, excellent. Or . . . ?

NONO: Or . . . non tantum!

PAOLINO: Brilliant! Or . . . ?

GIGLIO: Non modo, sir! I know, non modo or tantummodo!

Paolino furious. Shoving their heads back into the cupboard. Almost impossible until he kicks their feet from under them and slamming the door shut and locking it.

PAOLINO: You knew, you little buggers, you knew all the time.

His back to the door, the smiling half closed eyes of Nono looking at him. Mrs. Perella mouthing at him. Paolino looks as if he is going to go over the edge.

MRS.
PERELLA: Oh Lord, the downright shame of it. Here. I am here, while you . . . while boys jeer at me, while . . . while . . . oh the shame. It is now known that I visit you, the whole port will know . . .

PAOLINO: No no! Not you Nono, sit down. No.

Going over to comfort her.

You are here legit . . . er . . . properly, as the mother of a pupil. That's why I questioned Nono, here, and wasn't he good, how did he manage that? Good boy, Nono. No no, we're more likely to have trouble with my housekeeper, Rosaria, she's a real troublemaker that one.

MRS.
PERELLA: I know. The way she looked at me! The way she looked at me!

PAOLINO: The way she looked at me! No. You should not have come. I would have come to you.

MRS.
PERELLA: But the *Segesta* docks at five. I had to see you, to warn
            you, to tell you, and what I tell you is that there is no
            doubt, none, none at all. No doubt.

PAOLINO: Well!

MRS.
PERELLA: None.

PAOLINO: What is to be done? When does he sail?

MRS.
PERELLA: Tomorrow.

PAOLINO: Tomorrow?

MRS.
PERELLA: He'll do what he always does, gone tomorrow with the
            tide. For the East.

PAOLINO: No, he must not, he must . . . at least, at least . . . The
            East?

MRS.
PERELLA: Gone for two months. I'm finished, Paolino. Doomed.
            Ruined. Finished.

            *A knock on the door. Rosaria opens it and puts her
            head round, a ghastly smile.*

ROSARIA: Say if you would rather not, professor, but with your
            excellent permission I would care to get the key Toto
            left for his brother, the poor tired doctor. I left it on the
            table.

            *She has entered, tip-toed to the table, still with the
            ghastly smile on her face which says she knows
            something is going on but she doesn't yet know what.
            She picks up the key. Paolino takes it from her.*

PAOLINO: I'll give it to him.

ROSARIA: He wants it at once. He wants to go to sleep.

PAOLINO: Tell him I have it, would he be so kind as to wait?

ROSARIA: He's dead on his feet. Poor man, all night on the
            wards. Dead.

PAOLINO: Ask him to wait.

ROSARIA: Yes. All right. Yes, I will.

Exit Rosaria.

MRS.
PERELLA: What do you want with a doctor, Paolino?

PAOLINO: He's a friend. Advice. Help.

MRS.
PERELLA: For me?

PAOLINO: Yes.

MRS.
PERELLA: For pity's sake!

PAOLINO: Let me talk to him.

MRS.
PERELLA: I'd rather die.

PAOLINO: He's a friend, an intimate friend, more like a brother.

MRS.
PERELLA: You'll compromise me! Oh I would rather die, than this shame.

Then in her other voice:

What are you going to say to him?

PAOLINO: I don't know.

MRS.
PERELLA: You don't know!

PAOLINO: Something. I'll say something. You go, you and little Nono. What a lovely book, Nono, and you are enjoying it aren't you? My pleasure, don't thank me, there's no need, no need . . . Something, something. I'll come over before the *Segesta* docks.

To Nono.

It's yours, you may take it with you. And I'll come over to dine and I'll write in it for you if you like. What I'll say is: to little Nono, as a reward for his Latin studies. That should do the trick. Give me a . . . er . . . kiss.

MRS.
PERELLA: Say thank you to your teacher, Nono.

PAOLINO: Me.

NONO: There's no need.

MRS.
PERELLA: What do you mean, no need?

NONO: He said so. Didn't you?

PAOLINO: Perfectly true.

NONO: Shall you come to eat with us?

PAOLINO: I said so. With cakes. I shall bring cakes.

NONO: Good. See you soon.

PAOLINO: Soon.

MRS.
PERELLA: Something?

             She pleads as she is going.

PAOLINO: Yes I promise, something . . . keep your peck . . . er
             . . . chin up, chin up. See you soon.

MRS.
PERELLA: Soon, something . . .

             *Exit Mrs. Perella with Nono proudly carrying the
             book.
             Accompanied by Paolino.*

PAOLINO: Yes, something . . .

             *The stage remains empty a moment.
             Enter a yawn.
             A long racking seductive yawn. Behind the yawn
             Doctor Pulejo.
             Enter Paolino behind him, going to an armchair and
             swinging it forward for the doctor.*

PAOLINO: Here, here.

PULEJO: I need my bed.

PAOLINO: No. You can forget about sleep today.

PULEJO: Are you mad?

PAOLINO: I have a serious matter.

PULEJO: So have I, sleep.

PAOLINO: Are you a doctor?

> *Pulejo is a fine figure of a man, the same age as Paolino, he wears spectacles.*

PULEJO: Is this professional?

PAOLINO: It is.

PULEJO: A consultation?

PAOLINO: Yes.

> *Pulejo looks at his watch to time the start of the consultation and says:*

PULEJO: Very well.

> *Closing his eyes and swaying slightly.*

PAOLINO: It's a very serious matter.

PULEJO: Yes yes . . .

PAOLINO: Very serious.

PULEJO: Yes yes . . .

PAOLINO: You expect me to talk to you seriously when you're asleep on your feet and want to go to bed?

PULEJO: Yes yes . . .

PAOLINO: Wake up! I'm talking to you.

> *He shakes Pulejo who reacts angrily, looking at his watch still in his hand as if seeing it for the first time.*

PULEJO: I'm trying to sleep.

PAOLINO: You shouldn't be trying to sleep, I'm trying to consult you.

PULEJO: I've a right to sleep haven't I? All night . . .

PAOLINO: Yes, you've a right to sleep all night but not when I'm talking to you.

PULEJO: But you're not saying anything.

> *Pulejo making to go.*

PAOLINO: I'll get you a cup of coffee. Two cups.

PULEJO: I don't want coffee, I want bed.

PAOLINO: I'll jump off something and break a leg, two legs.

PULEJO: Brilliant, you'll force me to tend a broken leg, two legs but you won't spit out what you want to say.

PAOLINO: You'll have to stay.

PULEJO: Yes.

PAOLINO: And I'll talk, by God I'll talk.

PULEJO: Yes, but I won't be listening because I'll be concentrating on your broken leg, legs.

PAOLINO: You won't go to bed though.

PULEJO: And what will you gain? I'll get no sleep, you'll break your legs and the whole day will be wasted. Now, Paolino, just let me get a bit of shuteye and . . .

PAOLINO: No no no, there's not a moment to lose. You must help me.

PULEJO: What is it for heaven's sake?

PAOLINO: For heaven? Yes it is life and death!

PULEJO: It always is.

PAOLINO: Without your help I'm a dead man, washed, laid out, ready for my grave. Not just me, others, yes four others . . . no, I tell a lie, five, well almost five . . . shortly to be five . . . I shall kill the lot, the state I'm in, it'll be a shambles, the lot in bloody massacre. I need a remedy.

PULEJO: If there's something I can do, Paolino . . .

PAOLINO: Yes Nino, there is, perhaps.

PULEJO: All right, tell me . . .

PAOLINO: Are you paying attention?

PULEJO: Yes for God's sake, get . . .

PAOLINO: A brother, bear in mind I'm talking to you like a brother.

*Pulejo sits with a bump and yawns long and face
stretching. Paolino screams at him:*

Like a brother do you hear! No, not a brother, not just,
a doctor, because a doctor is like a priest in confession
isn't he?

PULEJO: We maintain professional . . .

PAOLINO: Good good. I speak to you under the seal of the
confessional . . .

PULEJO: You're an atheist aren't . . .

PAOLINO: I speak to you as to a brother and my priest.

*Paolino, to Pulejo's great amusement, strikes a solemn
pose, hand on stomach and says with great
dolorousness:*

Silent as the grave!

Pulejo caught in mid-yawn, splutters with laughter:

PULEJO: As the grave, as the grave, as the very grave . . . I'm
sorry. Yes. Agreed. As the grave.

PAOLINO: Nino!

*Paolino extends his hand with thumb and forefinger
joined, weighing his words.*

Nino, Perella has two houses.

PULEJO: Eh? Who's Perella?

PAOLINO: Captain Perella for fuck's sake!

*Then dropping his voice and shrinking from the
cupboard where labour Giglio and Belli:*

Perella of the General Navigation Line, deep sea
mariner, master of the *Segesta*. It's a ship.

PULEJO: All right, all right, Captain Perella, never heard of him.

PAOLINO: Good good good . . . nevertheless, silent as the grave,
eh? Two houses. One house here in Livorno, and
another house in Naples.

PULEJO: So?

PAOLINO: So? So . . . ! It's disgusting! A married man with a son takes advantage of the fact that he is a deep sea mariner to set up another house in another port with another woman, downright disgusting! I say so.

PULEJO: You do. But, where do you come into it? Is the wife of Captain Perella a relative or something?

From the cupboard a fusillade of knocks and the shouts of Giglio and Belli.

GIGLIO/
BELLI: Sir! Sir!

Paolino closes his eyes and without moving from where he stands shouts:

PAOLINO: What do you want?

Then eyes open to Pulejo:

I swear I'll do something drastic, something final . . . today. What do you want?

BELLI: We've finished, sir.

PAOLINO: You can't have, check it through.

GIGLIO: We've checked it through, sir.

PAOLINO: Then check it through again.

GIGLIO: We're suffocating in here, sir.

PAOLINO: Check it through again. Your hour's tuition is not up yet.

PULEJO: What are they doing in the cupboard?

PAOLINO: It's not a cupboard, it's a . . . box room.

BELLI: Open up, we can't breathe in here.

GIGLIO: Let us out!

PAOLINO: I'll be damned if I will. Be quiet!

Groans and silence.
Paolino back to Pulejo:

So, you say it shouldn't matter to me if Mrs. Perella isn't a relative? If she were?

PULEJO: Well, if she's a relative . . .

PAOLINO: She's not! What she is, doctor, is a poor woman
             suffering the torments of hell, a respectable woman . . .
             yes, betrayed in a vile way by her own husband! Does
             one have to be a relative to feel shock, indignation, that
             sort of thing . . . be sickened by it?

PULEJO: Yes. No . . . what can I do about it?

PAOLINO: Show some compassion for a start. That would be a
             help, doctor. Fine doctor you are, sitting there
             yawning, while I'm on tenterhooks . . . Can't you see I
             am? Give me your hand, doctor.

             *Paolino takes one of Pulejo's hands and grips it until
             Pulejo cries out in pain and astonishment.*

PULEJO: What are you doing! Let go . . . that was very painful.

PAOLINO: Did you feel it? I'm talking about feelings. Not the
             outside of people, doctor, not pictures moving across
             your field of vision. You're not interested in people as
             persons are you? Well, now you know what suffering is.
             Perhaps you'll now be able to feel their pain from the
             inside, put yourself in their shoes, make their anguish
             your own. Still hurt does it? Good.

PULEJO: I can feel pain thank you. I don't need to feel anybody
             else's pain to treat it; let everybody keep their own pain
             thank you very much . . . you know you're hilarious.

PAOLINO: Am I?

PULEJO: My dear chap, you're a scream.

PAOLINO: Makes you laugh does it? I know. Good stuff, very
             entertaining, sadness, fear, open display of emotions,
             even the most harrowing, despair, all that sort of thing,
             very funny, everybody laughs. Everybody cheers up.
             Good to see you laughing. What emotions you have, if
             you have any, you insulate with lies, conceal them, so
             you don't understand somebody like me who can't!
             Feel what I'm feeling, don't laugh, feel me inside
             yourself. I'm suffering.

PULEJO: What do you suffer from? All you talk about is Mrs.
             Perella . . .

PAOLINO: That's it, exactly. Her.

PULEJO: You suffer from Mrs. Perella . . .

PAOLINO: You've no idea how much. Listen, he's all right you
            say, two houses, dear old Captain Perella, two women,
            three or four children in Naples, one here, poor little
            Nono, he's all right. But he doesn't want any more
            children, Nino.

PULEJO: No, well five is plenty . . .

PAOLINO: He's only got one by his wife. The others are poor little
            bastards. He can get shot of poor little bastards can't
            he? That's what foundling homes are for. He can't
            shrug off another one here, can he, by his lawful
            wedded wife?

PULEJO: He most certainly can't.

PAOLINO: So what does he do, dear old Captain Perella, the rotten
            scoundrel? What does he do so that he shall not have
            another child by his wife, his only wife? He slams the
            bedroom door in her face! Whenever his ship docks
            here he is straight home, a damn good row on any
            pretext whatsoever and straight upstairs to sleep alone,
            the bolt on the door. That's been going on for three
            years. Next morning bright and early he sails with the
            tide, leaving . . . leaving . . . Mrs. Perella.

            Pulejo trying hard not to smile.

PULEJO: Door slammed in her face?

PAOLINO: Bolted. And the next day, gone.

PULEJO: Poor lady. Left . . . left . . . would you believe it?

PAOLINO: Is that it?

PULEJO: What?

PAOLINO: All you feel the need to say?

PULEJO: I'm sorry.

PAOLINO: You're sorry! What if she was your sister being left?
            Out of the bedroom.

PULEJO: Oh well, a relative, a sister . . . I'd knock seven colours
            of shit out of him, or so.

PAOLINO: You would?

PULEJO: Can't have that!

PAOLINO: Very well, now suppose this poor put upon lady has no
              brothers, has nobody who might with complete
              justification knock seven colours of shit out of her deep
              sea-going husband? To remind him of his duties. On
              land. Should this poor lady be left to suffer like this
              without a strong right arm raised in her . . . on her
              behalf? Is it just?

PULEJO: But, you . . .

PAOLINO: What about me?

PULEJO: Well to start with, how do you know these intimate
              details of . . .

PAOLINO: How do I know? How . . . ? I give Latin lessons to her
              son, his only son, poor lad, eleven years old. That's
              how. Lessons.

PULEJO: Ah, the penny's dropped. Saw them leave.

PAOLINO: You did not! Well, you did but . . . the grave, eh!
              Professional secrecy.

PULEJO: Oh yes. Oh yes, you may trust me.

PAOLINO: Not a word! She is virtue personified. The tears she
              has shed, the pity she has aroused in me, she is purity,
              she is goodness, she utters the noblest sentiments . . .
              and she's very beautiful too. Did you see?

PULEJO: No, she had her veil in place.

PAOLINO: I could understand it if she was ugly. But she is not,
              and she's still young. A woman of her beauty, youth,
              character discarded, rejected, deceived, tossed into the
              corner like an old boot. Who would not rebel? What
              woman would not? A woman of spirit and character
              . . . would you blame her, would you dare! Damn you,
              Pulejo, dare you to?

              *Pulejo reels back from the sudden intensity of Paolino's
              anger.*

PULEJO: Steady on.

PAOLINO: Would you? I'd like to see you try.

PULEJO: If it is true that her husband . . .

PAOLINO: Are you calling me a liar?

PULEJO: No. No, not at all.

PAOLINO: Then join me.

PULEJO: Join you?

PAOLINO: Stretch out your hand with mine to save her. For she sways on the edge of a precipice, stretch out your hand with mine . . . help me, help her, before she topples, plummets to the depths.

PULEJO: What precipice?

PAOLINO: She's been ignored by her husband for three years.

PULEJO: Dreadful. Yes?

PAOLINO: Well, can't you guess the nature of her precipice, a beautiful woman?

PULEJO: What?

Pulejo cold, severe.

PAOLINO: That's right, poor unfortunate . . . she is . . . finds herself . . .

PULEJO: No!

PAOLINO: What?

PULEJO: I won't do it. You can't make me. I want nothing to do with any criminal act.

Pulejo getting up to go.

PAOLINO: Sit down. What are you talking about? You utter idiot. You are you know. What do you imagine I want?

PULEJO: You tell me she's . . .

PAOLINO: Yes yes . . .

PULEJO: I'm a doctor . . .

PAOLINO: No thank you! She's a respectable lady. Virtue personified, I've told you once, virtue personified.

PULEJO: Well yes, point taken, jolly good but aren't you asking me to . . .

PAOLINO:	You scoundrel!
PULEJO:	That's a bit much . . .
PAOLINO:	What kind of a blackguard do you think I am? The very thought of what you're thinking revolts me, makes me sick.
PULEJO:	That's it. I come here a friend, a very tired friend, and I leave a scoundrel!

Getting up to go again.

A completely bewildered scoundrel. I give you one last chance to tell me what the hell you want from me. I cannot *understand* you!

PAOLINO:	I want what's right. I want what's honest and moral!
PULEJO:	There you go again. What?
PAOLINO:	I want our deep sea mariner to do his duty as a husband. Not slam and bolt the door in his wife's face when he comes ashore. Just once. Once will do.
PULEJO:	Aaaah! You want me to fix that. I'm to lead the Captain to the water and make him drink . . . Me . . .

Pulejo laughs, yawns, laughs, shakes his head wearily, his laughter almost hysterical.

PAOLINO:	Laugh! There is tragedy and you laugh! A woman's honour, life, at stake. Not to mention my life, your friend! And you laugh. What is so funny you pig, you? You don't realise there is only this one opportunity to grasp the nettle . . .

Renewed laughter from Pulejo.

Stop laughing you pig, you oaf, one night is all there is. Tonight. Tomorrow he's off on the high bloody seas again, gone for another two months at least, what then? He goes East, tomorrow. We've got one day . . .

PULEJO:	All right, all right . . .
PAOLINO:	I will kill you. You'll be the first to go of us all if you don't stop laughing. Quite horribly.
PULEJO:	I've stopped.

But he hasn't. He does however suppress it.

PAOLINO: Oh go on, laugh. Why not? Laugh at my despair. But help me. You're a doctor, you must know something.

PULEJO: That will stop him from quarrelling with his wife, and . . .

PAOLINO: Precisely.

PULEJO: For the best of all motives, morality!

PAOLINO: Stop laughing.

PULEJO: You just said I could.

PAOLINO: Yes, I'm sorry . . . yes.

PULEJO: How old is he?

PAOLINO: Older than her . . . me . . . us. Fortyish.

PULEJO: Ah, still in the er . . .

PAOLINO: A beast!

PULEJO: And been at sea three months?

PAOLINO: Yes, but he has put in at Naples, already, you see.

PULEJO: Naples, where he has the other . . .

PAOLINO: Exactly, the bastard! What he always does.

PULEJO: Naples first.

PAOLINO: Naples.

PULEJO: What we have to persuade him this evening is that he has duties here too.

PAOLINO: A wife.

PULEJO: Waiting for him?

PAOLINO: Do you doubt it?

PULEJO: No no, but might there not be more to it than that?

PAOLINO: What more? There is nothing more. There is nothing here but Captain Perella's unforgivably rotten behaviour and the consequences thereof.

PULEJO: Consequences which you may have contributed to . . .

PAOLINO: We didn't intend to! There must be intention before blame can be attributed, mere chance won't do. So where does the blame lie? With whom? It's as if you owned a plot of land you didn't plant, you let it go, but on that plot of land there's a struggling young fruit tree which blossoms miraculously and bears fruit. Somebody comes along and picks a fruit, eats it, throws away the stone, fruit that nobody wanted, a stone thrown away and nobody cares. One day a tree grows from the stone, on abandoned land, did the eater of the fruit intend that it should? He did not. Nor did the abandoned earth which received the stone. So, to whom does this new tree belong? To you, the owner of the land. You're to blame.

PULEJO: Me? No thank you.

PAOLINO: Then cultivate your land! Look after it, tend it, plant it. Don't let complete strangers pick fruit from your abandoned tree!

PULEJO: I won't. Tell him that, your deep sea captain. He should cultivate his land.

PAOLINO: He must. He must do it.

PULEJO: We'll do our best to see that he does.

PAOLINO: Nino! You're an angel . . .

Paolino kisses him.

. . . thank you, thank you! How?

PULEJO: Does he eat at home?

PAOLINO: Yes, dinner at six, I'm invited.

PULEJO: Good. You won't arrive empty handed?

PAOLINO: Empty handed? I most certainly will.

PULEJO: Take something.

PAOLINO: I promised cakes, I didn't mean it but I promised cakes.

PULEJO: Go and buy the cakes.

PAOLINO: What are you going to do?

PULEJO: Take them to my brother Toto at the pharmacy. While you do that I'll have a wash and a shave . . .

PAOLINO: No you won't. I'm not letting you out of my sight.

PULEJO: Go and buy the cakes. My key please.

PAOLINO: The cakes are for the boy.

PULEJO: Yes but you'll all want to taste them won't you, the lady and the captain, not you . . .

PAOLINO: Not me?

PULEJO: Well you can if you like, but come straight back home. The key please? To my house.

PAOLINO: You'll go straight to bed. No.

PULEJO: No I won't. I'm well and truly awake now. I've got house calls to do.

PAOLINO: You can wash and shave here.

PULEJO: Give me my bloody key!

PAOLINO: All right. I trust you. It is life and death Nino, mind. What are you going to put into the cakes?

PULEJO: Better that you shouldn't know.

PAOLINO: Is it possible to . . . er . . . can you scientifically . . . ? Oh God!

PULEJO: What's wrong now?

PAOLINO: It stinks, that's what's wrong.

PULEJO: Well . . .

PAOLINO: You think you know me very well, you see me as nothing more than some fool who has got himself in a mess, don't you? Well, I'm not . . . not just that. You use science, make a living out of it, but I love science impartially. That it should come to this! Me using science for this. Scientific knowledge has been gained by sacrifice. I revere science!

PULEJO: Oh well, if you regard it as sacrilege . . .

PAOLINO: No. Don't please take it badly. I just hate having to do it, Nino, for something like this. I'm eaten up inside

my dear fellow, I really am, but I'll do it. This has all
come about because I took pity on a woman in tears,
asked her how, asked her what, asked her who . . . she
didn't want to tell me, I pressed her and then she did,
and I gave her comfort, the best way I could, and there
I was, in a jam. And you're laughing. I know it's
ridiculous. But don't blame me, blame the harsh
mocking cruelty of that husband of hers. Yes, I'm
ridiculous and you laugh at me, just because I want
that bloody man . . .

PULEJO: To get in there and do his duty as a husband and sea
            captain.

PAOLINO: Yes. That's all I can want. That's all I'm allowed to
            want.

PULEJO: Morality strikes.

PAOLINO: Not my morality, yours, theirs, it's how you, they want
            it. Left to me I'd kill him. And what's more I will,
            does he not buckle to and do it. I will so help me. I
            beg you to believe me when I tell you that I'm an
            honourable man, it's true, and I'd marry her in a trice,
            tomorrow, do the right thing tomorrow if I could . . .
            yes. What do you think? Will twenty be enough?

PULEJO: Twenty what?

PAOLINO: Cakes for God's sake, how many cakes do you want?
            Twenty?

PULEJO: More than enough.

PAOLINO: Are you sure? I'll get more, thirty.

            Exit Pulejo.

            Forty or so . . .

            *Paolino following him when all hell breaks loose in the
            cupboard.*

GIGLIO/
BELLI: Sir! Sir! Open the door. You can't leave us here!

            *Paolino opens the cupboard door and the boys tumble
            out, books and boys across the floor.*

PAOLINO: Yes.

GIGLIO: It's wrong, sir. It's wrong, we nearly died in there.

BELLI: You're a bully, sir. I'm going to ask my parents to take
               me away. At once.

               *Paolino looks at the struggling, furious, exhausted boys
               throwing their books from them, dishevelled, in tears
               and says distractedly:*

PAOLINO: I *am* sorry. Do forgive me.

               Exit Paolino.
               *Bleat and chatter, bleat and chatter and then exit
               Giglio and Belli.*

ACT TWO

The sound of seagulls.

Scene: House of Captain Perella in Leghorn 1919.

> *The house of a deep sea mariner, with objects brought back from the Seven Seas, marine pictures, old photographs on the walls.*
> *From a verandah a view of the sea and the harbour.*
> *A plant stand with five pot plants.*
> *Doors to the Captain's bedroom and to other rooms of the house and hall.*
> *China cabinet, sideboard, a divan.*
> *The table laid for dinner for four, an elaborate setting.*
> *Late afternoon.*
>
> *Enter Nono looking through his exercise book.*
> *Enter Paolino to beam on him in desperation.*

PAOLINO: First thing you must do, Nono, is show your father your exercise book, your excellent marks.

NONO: Yes, great . . .

> *Nono looks more closely at his book and then at Paolino, showing him.*
> *Paolino makes a great gesture, whips out his red pencil, changes the mark.*

PAOLINO: You are so right Nono, whatever was I thinking of? That translation is worth a nine if anything is . . . there.

NONO: So, two nines. So, that's three eights, one ten and two nines!

PAOLINO: Show him your excellent marks at once. Today you must do your very best to please your father.

NONO: Of course.

> *Nono counting on his fingers.*

PAOLINO: You must take care not to annoy him. He is in port after a long sea voyage . . .

NONO: Naples . . .

PAOLINO: That's right, Naples . . . but before that probably America . . . what are you counting?

NONO: Ssssssssh! Three . . .

Nono is counting by holding the fingers of his left hand, three, with his right.

Then four, five . . .

Five fingers of the left hand.

. . . six, seven . . .

Thumb and forefinger of the right hand.

. . . eight, nine, ten . . .

Counting off the last three fingers of the right hand.

. . . makes half a lire. Half a lire!

PAOLINO: Eh? What do you mean half a lire?

NONO: What I get. Great. Papa gives a soldo for every eight I get, three eights is three soldi, two soldi for every nine and you've given me two of those so that's another four soldi, right? I get three soldi for a ten. Three, four and three come to ten, which is half a lire. Half a lire! Half a lire! Half a lire!

PAOLINO: Oh good. That's good. Are you pleased? You're pleased.

NONO: Half a lire! Half a lire!

PAOLINO: I'm so pleased.

NONO: He won't be . . .

PAOLINO: Why will he not?

NONO: He gets very angry.

PAOLINO: Why?

NONO: Used to give me more, three for a nine, five for a ten. That was before you started casting eights, nines and tens to the winds . . .

PAOLINO: I did what?

NONO: That's what he said, to the winds. He grabbed my
book, threw it in the air, like this, shouting.

PAOLINO: He got angry?

NONO: Livid. To the winds, this teacher casts eights, nines,
tens to the winds. Up in the air.

PAOLINO: I don't, you're very clever.

NONO: He put the going rate down. He was in a rage. He said
my God. Up in the air!

*Nono tosses the book up in the air and behind him.
Paolino catches, scrabbles for it.*

PAOLINO: In that case, we don't want him angry, do we?

Red pencil out, changing the marks.

Five, six . . . another five . . .

NONO: You can't do that! Half a lire!

PAOLINO: I'll give you half a lire.

Paolino digging in his purse.

NONO: No no . . . !

PAOLINO: What do you mean no no, er . . . Nono?

NONO: No!

Nono standing teeth gritted, eyes closed, fists clenched.

PAOLINO: All the same where you get it from surely, me or your
father?

NONO: No!

PAOLINO: My one wish is to make your father happy after his
long sea voyage but, if it's going to make him go off the
deep end, er . . . instead, we can't have that . . . can
we?

NONO: I want my three eights, my two nines, and my ten what
I got, that's what.

*Nono stamps his feet on the spot in his rage, fists tight
clenched still.
Then stops.*

PAOLINO: Truth to tell you do not deserve them, Nono.

             Nono opens his eyes, glares:

NONO: I do, I do!

             Then asks cunningly:

             Why did you give me them then?

PAOLINO: I didn't know you were making your father angry. I
             didn't know you were making him cough up for high
             marks, that's too much. Today of all days we must all
             be happy . . . you too with your half a lire.

             *The money found, offered, and to the great relief of
             Paolino accepted by Nono.*

             Not a word to papa? Our secret? Now, I'm giving it to
             you because although you do not deserve all those nines
             and tens you do deserve something for making good
             progress. You are coming on.

NONO: Like you wrote in the scary insect book?

PAOLINO: Certainly. Yes. Just what I wrote in the picture book I
             gave you.

             *Enter Grazia. She is old, churlish, has a face like a
             horse and moves like a tired old drayhorse, head down
             and unstoppable but very very slow.*

GRAZIA: Isn't she here?

PAOLINO: She's in there, Grazia.

             *Pointing to where Mrs. Perella prepares herself for the
             coming of her sea captain husband.
             Grazia points herself in the direction of the room, then,
             too much for her, she indicates Nono:*

GRAZIA: Then he can go and tell her that he's come. The sailor.

NONO: Papa's here! I'm going on board.

             *A dash for the door, arm caught by Paolino who
             swings him back.*

PAOLINO: Wait. Your mother must be told first.

NONO: She knows. I always go.

PAOLINO: Grazia, please go and inform madam.

GRAZIA: Tell her?

             *Grazia pointing herself in the direction of the door to
             Mrs. Perella and starting.*

NONO: She knows.

GRAZIA: Tell her? I'll tell her, I'll tell her. What a to-do!

             *Reaching the door and putting up a hand to knock and
             pushing with her advancing foot at the same time,
             going straight in.*
             Exit Grazia.
             Nono at the door to the hall shouts:

NONO: Sailor! Come here! Look lively now!

             Enter Filippo, the sailor, very much the "old salt".

FILIPPO: Look lively? He's a caution is the young admiral.

             *Arms open, crouching to catch and inviting Nono to
             throw himself into them.*

             Aren't you now?

NONO: You, sailor! Take me to papa at once!

FILIPPO: Aye aye admiral, soon as we gets leaf to sail.

             *Enter Mrs. Perella who has been dressing with extreme
             care and concentration and consequently looks
             extraordinary.*
             The sailor removes his hat.
             Nono sits on his shoulders, jerking up and down.

             At your service, ma'am, Mrs. Captain. Got the boy
             inboard, permission to make way?

MRS.
PERELLA: Is my husband's ship docking?

FILIPPO: Approaching its berth ma'am, Mrs. Captain, I came
             ashore prior, by now she should be hard on.

NONO: Come on! I want to see it.

FILIPPO: You shall admiral, some time yet before she ties up,
             she's a stiff ship the *Segesta*, takes some handling.

MRS.
PERELLA: I put him in your care, Filippo.

FILIPPO: That's right, ma'am, you may do that, avast jerking
                admiral or you'll sink old Filippo.

                Exit Filippo ridden by Nono.
                Paolino contemplates Mrs. Perella who colours in
                embarrassment under his gaze.

PAOLINO: What have you got on?

MRS.
PERELLA: Oh!

PAOLINO: Yes.

MRS.
PERELLA: Won't it do? You can't realise what it has cost me to do
                this.

PAOLINO: Heart, I do, I do, but it won't.

MRS
PERELLA: Why will it not?

PAOLINO: Only One, not enough.

MRS.
PERELLA: I can do no more. Modesty forbids I do more.

PAOLINO: For heaven's sake woman, he arrives any moment! He
                must be struck! His first sight of you must do the trick.
                Sweetheart, I know you've tried. You have no allure.

MRS.
PERELLA: Guide me, how should I be?

PAOLINO: I know the torment your chaste and pure soul is
                undergoing. I know what it costs you to set out to
                deliberately inflame a beast like your husband . . . I
                know. You have to go further. Make further sacrifice.
                The whole . . . hog.

MRS.
PERELLA: More . . . décolleté?

PAOLINO: The whole boiling. Much much more.

MRS.
PERELLA: My God! Please . . . no.

PAOLINO: I beg you. Your body is a shrine encrusted with
              precious jewels, locked, undiscovered, chastely hidden,
              but you must let go just a little.

MRS.
PERELLA: What are you saying?

PAOLINO: Scruples out the window.

MRS.
PERELLA: He's never taken any notice anyway.

PAOLINO: He must be forced to. The man is an animal, animals
              look for display, they cannot understand modest pure
              beauty. Concealed treasures mean nothing to them. Let
              me do it . . .

              Paolino reaches out his hands.
              Mrs. Perella leaps back, her hands on her chest.

MRS.
PERELLA: He knows what I've got . . . !

              Paolino exasperated:

PAOLINO: Jog his memory.

MRS.
PERELLA: He isn't interested.

PAOLINO: I know my only One, but that's because you don't
              know how to use them.

MRS.
PERELLA: Use them?

PAOLINO: To your advantage. I admire it myself, it earns my love
              and my esteem and my respect, it is what I like about
              you; you don't know, whereas other women know very
              well what to do with them.

              Mrs. Perella asking, shocked:

MRS.
PERELLA: What? What do they . . . do?

PAOLINO: Do? Very little . . . they don't hide the damn things is
              what they do!

MRS.
PERELLA: Oh!

PAOLINO: Forgive me but you're driving me to it. How do you think I feel? I'm a man of sensitivity, what sort of sacrifice am I making? I don't like having to explain these things to you, ruining your innocence, nor do I like the idea of tarting you up for another man.

Hands in the air, straight up from the position they have been since she moved from them when they were indicating her charms.
He shouts:

Putting virtue on display for the beast! It is vile. But, got to be, no time to lose, we must, to save you . . . and me. Take your blouse OFF!

MRS.
PERELLA: Off?

PAOLINO: Off! Wrong colour, not going to a funeral . . . funereal colour, purple . . . yet, are we? You need something will scream at him. Red will.

MRS.
PERELLA: I haven't got red.

PAOLINO: That Japanese silk . . .

MRS.
PERELLA: High neckline.

PAOLINO: Then get it down, girl! Easy, lower, fold it back and stitch a bit of lace to it, lower, right down . . . there's a good girl . . . you want it down to here at least.

His pointing finger.
Mrs. Perella reacts to it as if it were red hot metal.

MRS.
PERELLA: No!

PAOLINO: Yes.

MRS.
PERELLA: As low as that?

PAOLINO: Believe me. Take my advice.

MRS.
PERELLA: Not that low. Never!

PAOLINO: There is no point in anything higher. Your hair! Curls,
                you need curls, like hooks, one in the middle of your
                forehead like a hook, one on each cheek . . .

MRS.
PERELLA: Hooks?

PAOLINO: Curls. If you can't do it I'll do it for you. I will. Curls
                like upside-down question marks, one here, one here,
                one here . . .

                His finger like a hook in each position.

MRS.
PERELLA: Why?

PAOLINO: Because I say so! That's why . . . go and do it, get this
                off, curl your hair and low, remember very low.

                Pushing her towards her room.
                Exit Mrs. Perella, leaving the door open.
                Paolino looks at the table set for dinner, his face
                twisted, trying to imagine what Perella will want, will
                expect.

                How does one anticipate the needs of a wild beast?

                He takes the flowers out and makes to throw them
                away, then sticks them back into the vase again, and
                gathers up more from other vases, cramming them in.

                Sentiment, sentiment, they love sentiment.

                A squeak from Mrs. Perella off.

MRS.
PERELLA: Ouch!

PAOLINO: What have you done?

MRS.
PERELLA: My finger! With a pin.

PAOLINO: Do you bleed?

MRS.
PERELLA: The blood has drained from me!

PAOLINO: I know my love, you could do with some colour in your
                cheeks.

MRS.
PERELLA: Shame will do that!

PAOLINO: Don't count on it. Fear may drive the gentle blush of shame from your cheeks. Rouge is the answer. I have it.

> *A parcel in his pocket, he puts it near.*
> *Mrs. Perella weeps.*

You weep?

MRS.
PERELLA: Oh God! Oh God!

PAOLINO: Have you pricked yourself some more?

> *Paolino looks through into the room, comes out hastily.*

She's got that mouth open again. Awful. He'll know, he'll know at once.

> *Paolino opening the parcel, a new pot of rouge, a brush etc.*
> *Enter Grazia.*

GRAZIA: He's here.

PAOLINO: Who?

GRAZIA: The gentleman you expect.

PAOLINO: With cakes? Tell him to come in. The pharmacist, Grazia.

GRAZIA: In here?

PAOLINO: Yes, quickly, let him in.

GRAZIA: Quickly? In here?

PAOLINO: If you don't mind.

GRAZIA: Who cares do I mind? If you say . . .

> *Grazia on her laborious way, her feet like the feet of the drayhorse lifted up and placed down almost delicately.*

. . . in here, then in here he comes and that's all there is to it.

PAOLINO: Yes you're so right, I'm sorry, if you'd be so kind . . .

GRAZIA: Kind? Mind? What a fuss, what a to-do.

> *Exit Grazia.*
> *Paolino closes his eyes and tries to bring on a state of calm,*
> *saying:*

PAOLINO: The most important thing is for you to keep your
temper, Paolino. I think so.

> *Opening his eyes and like he has had an electric shock,*
> *throwing himself at the open door to the room where*
> *Mrs. Perella prepares herself to tell her:*

The cakes are here!

> *Enter a cake, in a box, followed by the finger and the*
> *arm and the whole of Toto.*

Where the hell have you been?

TOTO: It took longer.

PAOLINO: Much.

TOTO: I hope you don't mind me saying this but I have it on
my conscience that there is a person who in all
innocence . . . indeed he is an innocent party in this
. . . the . . .

PAOLINO: Innocent? He's not innocent, he won't do his duty, he
must be made to, he's not innocent he's guilty as sin of
depreciation, of dereliction, neglect . . . infraction not
innocence! My heart is a ticking bomb, I am packed
with the explosives of emotion, rage, anguish, despair!
You throw me innocence, that word. I am an honest
man, I have shouted the truth from the house tops no
matter what, you know that and here I am compelled
to resort to duplicity with an imbecile like you!
Innocence! Captain Perella is not innocent.

TOTO: Is there not a child in the house?

PAOLINO: Not yet there isn't but there will be very soon if . . .
oh, you mean the boy? I suppose so. You might call
him innocent.

TOTO: I thought, well, a boy in the house, well . . . heaven
forbid that . . .

PAOLINO: Yes, I see what you mean.

TOTO: We are responsible people, my brother the doctor and I
           . . . we could not have the boy . . . and who can tell?
           With the best will in the wor . . .

PAOLINO: What have you done . . .

           *Glaring at the small cake box held by Toto as if seeing
           it for the first time.*

           . . . with my cakes?

TOTO: Eaten them.

PAOLINO: All forty!

TOTO: Half. The rest I've left for my brother to have with his
           supper.

PAOLINO: What is that?

TOTO: Chocolate and cream gâteau, very nice. Delicious.
           Scrumptious.

PAOLINO: Don't try to tempt me you fool. This isn't a bloody
           party for me.

TOTO: I had to make it. Look . . .

           Toto opens the box, shows Paolino.

           . . . couldn't have cakes, little fingers picking up cakes
           . . . see, there can be no mistake, half white, half
           chocolate, it's in the chocolate. The boy may have the
           white half, and you if you want some. It's the chocolate
           he must eat.

PAOLINO: Chocolate for the captain. Will it . . . ?

TOTO: Oh yes, yes, yes, yes! Fear not.

PAOLINO: My dear friend.

TOTO: Of course.

PAOLINO: His ship has docked.

TOTO: Excellent.

PAOLINO: Fingers crossed.

TOTO: It's in the bag.

PAOLINO: What do you mean?

TOTO: Do you doubt it?

PAOLINO: Toto . . . one cup, every morning. You may count on
             it.

TOTO: Thank you, Paolino.

PAOLINO: Go, there's a good chap.

TOTO: Of course.

             Exit Toto.
             Paolino picks up the cake and advances towards the
             table, the cake held in his hands like an offering.
             He genuflects at the table and then elevates it like a
             consecrated host saying:

PAOLINO: Out of the depths I cry to you oh Lord, make it work!
             At stake is a woman's life and honour and the fate of a
             family and . . . my own unworthy life, not least my
             own life.

             Then places it in the centre of the table.
             Stands back from the altar of the Beast to scrutinise,
             genuflects again.
             Enter Mrs. Perella.

MRS.
PERELLA: I could die, I am so ashamed!

             She has entered so very silently, her hands over her
             chest, her eyes lowered, in the throes of the most
             hideous embarrassment and shame, three kiss curls and
             extreme décolleté.

PAOLINO: Your hands. Let me see.

MRS.
PERELLA: No, please.

PAOLINO: What is the use of pricking your finger to lower your
             neckline if you keep your hands over? He's got to see.

MRS.
PERELLA: Please no.

PAOLINO: You must show him. Remove your hands.

             Mrs. Perella does, to her face; bursting into tears.

             Tears! A magnificent touch . . . excellent but don't ruin

your eyes . . . don't. Wonderful. Don't cry. I'm sorry
my love. I have to tell you that I suffer more. This
hurts me more than it hurts you. I would face death
rather than have your virtue offered up on the altar of
the Beast, I am in agony that you have to prostitute
yourself in this way.

MRS.
PERELLA: And it will all be for nothing! Oooooooooooooooooh
               nothing!

PAOLINO: See it as your holy martyrdom, take strength from
               those that have walked the path before, allow me to try
               to give you courage. Smile. I can give you strength.
               Smile. Force a little smile, come on, there's a good girl,
               smile. We'll get nowhere if you can't smile at him.

MRS.
PERELLA: I have forgotten how to smile.

PAOLINO: It's easy, look.

               *He stands very still for a moment and then grimaces at
               her.*

               See? Now you try.

MRS.
PERELLA: I can't.

PAOLINO: Yes you can. Look at me, I'm a monkey, yes?

               *He capers, arms long, head scratched, arms swinging
               near the floor.*

               Animals make you laugh. Everybody laughs at animals.
               A cat? On all fours, that's funny isn't it? You're
               laughing, I know you're laughing, a monkey and a
               cat . . .

               *Mrs. Perella still crying but now trying to laugh at the
               same time.*

               Come on, smile, laugh . . . a mountain goat, they leap
               don't they? I shall leap. Like a mountain goat.

               He does.

               Animals are very funny, three cheers for animals, hip

hip, hip hip, hooray for animals, soon forget your
worries . . . animals! There you are, you're laughing!

Mrs. Perella is in hysterics.

MRS.
PERELLA: Stop, please stop, it's awful, please.

She dissolves in tears again, great sobs.

PAOLINO: And you were beginning to laugh so nicely! What is the
matter with you? Stop it for Christ's sake. Stop it!
You'll drive me crazy. You will. This is enough,
woman!

*He grabs her and shakes her hard, brutally, angrily, so
that she is stunned into silence.*

Stop it. Stand up straight and stop it. Stand still.
Silence! Not a quiver of a lip, nothing. That's better.
Now I shall paint your face.

MRS.
PERELLA: Paint it?

PAOLINO: Not a word!

*Holding her up, and turning from her to reach for the
cosmetics he has brought, turning back to her as she lets
out a little whimper:*

MRS.
PERELLA: But . . .

PAOLINO: Not a sound, that lip . . . still. Dry your eyes, cheeks, I
shall paint them. You are pale as death, delicate blue
and dove white, eggshell china . . . we cannot expect
the Beast to come near to appreciating your beauty, the
gentleness of your melancholy charm . . . paint, head
up . . .

*He takes hold of her chin and turns her face to his charged
brush.*

. . . for the Beast you must look like one of those
women.

MRS.
PERELLA: Oh!

PAOLINO: You must and so . . . the cheeks, and so, and so . . .
             hide behind it, thick and lurid . . . and so, this he will
             understand. The mouth, open, open . . . so the mouth,
             like a huge red fruit, luscious, don't cry don't cry you'll
             ruin it, the paint will run . . . Eyes, shadows for your
             eyes, I have all the colours, a palette of colours, close
             your eyes, and so, and so and your eyebrows, dark
             eyebrows, they have dark eyebrows no matter the
             colour of their hair . . . there, and so. Let me see? Yes.
             That will do the trick.

             *Mrs. Perella looks frightful though she might look
             enticing in the semi-darkness of a brothel.*

             He cannot now prefer his tart in Naples, our sordid sea
             captain, just let him see you!

             *Mrs. Perella stands in shock, like a puppet, a bawdy
             fairground puppet.*

             See what you think.

             *Paolino holds a mirror up for her.
             She gasps in horror.*

             But that's it. This is how you must look for him.

MRS.
PERELLA: It's not me.

PAOLINO: It is the new you.

MRS.
PERELLA: It's a horrible mask.

PAOLINO: Which you must wear for him.

MRS.
PERELLA: He won't recognise me.

PAOLINO: He must not. That is the point.

MRS.
PERELLA: Paolino, I'm a mother!

PAOLINO: My poor dear heart, you are right. I swear I weep
             myself.

             *He puts his arms around her, real tenderness and
             whispers to her.*

What can you do? This is what he wants, this is how he wants you, this is how he would have you, not as a mother, not he to his shame, not he. You face him with this mask, your protection against his beastliness, whilst behind it you are still yourself, inviolate, suffering for us both, for our love.

Nono heard off: "Vwhoooooo! Vwhooooo . . ."
Paolino releases Mrs. Perella quickly.

NONO: *(Off)* Here's Papa! Here's Papa . . .

PAOLINO: He's here.

MRS.
PERELLA: Oh God, God, God, God . . .

PAOLINO: Smile, remember . . . smile . . .

MRS.
PERELLA: . . . God, God, God, God . . .

PAOLINO: . . . please smile!

NONO: *(Off)* Here's Papa . . . here's pa . . .

Enter Nono sprawling from the boot of Captain Perella.
Enter Captain Perella.

PERELLA: Shut up, I don't need it!

Captain Perella is like a boar, huge, bristling, his eyes so deep in his face and hair that one only knows of his regard from the direction of his great bulb of a nose. Nono picked up by Mrs. Perella and Paolino.

MRS.
PERELLA: Oh poor Nono.

PAOLINO: Poor boy, are you hurt, Nono?

PERELLA: Not him.

Another shove of a kick at Nono.

Shut that noise! You, professor, don't know. My father took me by the scruff of my neck when I was six to punish me for not learning how to swim. He held me in the air, kicking. Then he threw me from the jetty into the sea, fully dressed to my boots, shouting: "Sink or swim!" Scarf, hat, boots, overcoat, sink or swim.

PAOLINO: What happened?

PERELLA: I didn't sink. I don't agree with your methods, professor.

PAOLINO: You don't?

PERELLA: I do not.

PAOLINO: Why?

PERELLA: Too bloody soft if you really want to know and that's a fact, won't do! You spoil the little turd.

Paolino splutters in astonishment.

PAOLINO: Me? I do not. The fact is, if you want facts . . . I can be, if need be, believe me . . .

PERELLA: Need be? Wouldn't do at sea, need be. They need toughening or they sink. He's a spoilt brat, that's why he gets my boot up his bent end.

PAOLINO: He may well be spoiled but there is very good reason why . . . and it isn't me . . . it's . . .

PERELLA: His silly bloody mother? Thought it was.

PAOLINO: No! Not her . . .

Paolino becomes heatedly involved.

. . . she . . . his mother is a perfect mother. I will give you the reason. It is inevitable that he should appear spoiled, he is an only child.

PERELLA: Balls! Anyway, only child, that's what you think.

PAOLINO: I beg your pardon, is he not?

Perella dismisses the question angrily:

PERELLA: It's upbringing does it. How they're brought up!

PAOLINO: Undoubtedly. But were there two children, captain . . .

PERELLA: That's enough of that, professor. Never say that again, not even as a joke. One is more than enough for me!

*Nono has run to his mother. He has stopped dead at
the sight of her.
He is astonished, frightened.
She wrings her hands, begging him with her eyes not to
shout out in his fear and amazement.
She opens her mouth.
Nono shaking his hands at the wrists in his agitation,
starting to make the sounds he does when his mother
opens her mouth, "Op op op . . ."*

PAOLINO: Please, captain I would not wish to annoy you, not at
all . . . but it is generally thought that . . .

NONO: Op op op . . .

PERELLA: Not by me, professor. Another child is *not* what I need.

NONO: Op op op op op op . . .

PERELLA: Stop that noise . . .

*Captain Perella about to give Nono a back hander
when he sees his wife for the first time properly.
A roar of laughter.*

What do you look like!

Roars of laughter.

What on earth have you done to yourself, is it you? It
can't be you. What have you got on? You've terrified
the child, look at him, as if he's seen a . . . seen a . . .

*Near helpless with laughter, the captain staggers over
to his wife to pull her hands away from her chest, her
mouth.
Paolino, his hands working, as if he could strangle
Perella in his helplessness did he not restrain himself.*

What a fright you look. Have you seen her? Look at
her. All we need is the organ grinder, eh? Da da da da
dada . . . Uuuuuuugh, look at that. What have you
done? Plenty there to catch cold. What? Eh? Can you
believe what you see, professor? Like the organ
grinder's monkey, where's your tail? Eh? Does it not
shock you, professor?

PAOLINO: Not at all . . .

PERELLA: Does me, and I've seen some sights.

PAOLINO: All I can see is that your wife seems to have taken
              some care . . .

PERELLA: Care? She's unrecognisable. She's got the whole lot on
              the slab, well, nigh on!

MRS.
PERELLA: Francesco . . . I thought . . . I've tried . . . !

PERELLA: You have. Close the shop. I'm not interested.

              His laughter stops as suddenly as it started.
              Turning from her to Paolino.

              No good to me any more, I wouldn't even cross the
              road for it. Couldn't raise my hand to it any more, let
              alone anything else. Eh? Haven't had my tongue down
              a throat in years!

              Then back to his wife.

              Go and wash your face, my dear, thank you very much
              for the thought, now I'm starving. You starving? I'm
              eating straight away, professor.

MRS.
PERELLA: Everything is ready, Francesco.

PERELLA: Of course it is. You eating with us, professor? Sit
              down.

PAOLINO: Yes, yes . . . I think so.

MRS.
PERELLA: I have already invited him, Francesco.

PERELLA: Sit down then.

              Captain Perella already at the table, sitting, grabbing
              a napkin, sticking it in his tunic collar.

              Right. I like my grub. Lots of it. I don't care what
              anybody thinks, they can take offence if they like. I eat
              a lot and I enjoy eating and it shows.

              A belch and a pat of his paunch.
              He grimaces as Mrs. Perella makes to sit opposite him.

              No! If you won't wash your face then you must not sit

opposite me, put me off my food. Worse thing you can do, laugh and eat, you get it going down the wrong way. What put the idea into your head to tart yourself up like that?

MRS.
PERELLA: Nothing, nothing . . . in particular.

PERELLA: I'm laughing again. Just like that? Look at her, professor. How can you seriously contemplate . . .

PAOLINO: I think she looks . . . splendid! I think you ought to admit that, captain.

PERELLA: I am trying to understand you, professor. Yes. If she was another sort of woman, yes, she might be considered . . . splendid. I'll give you that but, not a wife. Eh? A certain sort of woman . . . if you know what I mean . . . well yes. But a wife just looks funny. It's no good, I can't take it seriously, I can't help laughing, change places with her, come on, you get up and let the professor sit opposite. You've got to admit it, she just looks funny. Change places!

PAOLINO: I don't mind, whatever you wish.

PERELLA: Thank you. So where's the food?

Nono sitting on the divan, curled up, sulking.

Nono! Dinner.

NONO: No, I don't want any, no no.

PERELLA: At once!

The table leaps as Captain Perella hits it with his fist.

Up here! To the table. Do as you're told and don't answer back.

PAOLINO: Come on little Nono . . .

PERELLA: Come on little Nono! That's enough, professor. Nono!

Fist again on the table.

No persuasion. He must do as he's told and jump to it. Nono!

Perella lurches from his chair and lifts Nono by the

> *scruff of his neck holding him up.*
> *Mrs. Perella and Paolino quietly sobbing and*
> *whispering urgently:*

MRS.
PERELLA: Oh God . . .

PAOLINO: Be patient . . . smile . . . look, remember?

> *Paolino puts his face into the smile.*

PERELLA: Down!

> *Captain Perella dumps Nono into the chair.*

You'll sit there, up straight. Sit up straight!

> *Nono terrified straightens up.*

Nothing to eat, as a punishment.

> *Enter Grazia with a soup tureen. She will serve the*
> *meal from the sideboard.*

Are we going to eat or not, woman?

MRS.
PERELLA: We are, we are . . .

PERELLA: Then where is it? We are, we are.

MRS.
PERELLA: Here it is Francesco . . .

PERELLA: About bloody time!

> *Perella looks at Paolino who still has the smile on his*
> *face.*
> *He snorts, snuffles, growls and warns:*

Professor, do me a favour, a great favour, and I speak
to you as a friend; don't smile when I'm giving my wife
or my son a bollocking, right?

PAOLINO: I?

PERELLA: Wipe it off. You're still smiling.

PAOLINO: Am I?

PERELLA: Yes you are. Smiling.

PAOLINO: I swear to you captain I didn't know. Don't know . . .

I must be someone else because I swear to you I am not smiling.

PERELLA: Stripe me! Of course you are. You are bloody well smiling . . .

PAOLINO: Still? Oh dear, this is serious, because I'm not, really. The last thing in the world I feel like doing at the moment is smile . . . if I am smiling then I am in the grip of my nerves, they are doing it of their own accord.

Grazia has served soup.

Yes.

PERELLA: Your nerves make you smile do they?

PAOLINO: Yes, that must be it, smiling nerves.

PERELLA: Mine don't.

PAOLINO: Funny thing, to tell you the truth, mine don't usually . . . must be one of those days . . . nerves!

Perella eating his soup noisily.

NONO: Can I eat, papa?

PERELLA: Who gave him that?

MRS.
PERELLA: Grazia, she . . .

PERELLA: She shouldn't have!

MRS.
PERELLA: Perhaps she didn't know.

PERELLA: You should have told her.

To Nono.

All right, get it down you, just this once, mind. Go on!

Nono wriggles, not touching his soup.

What's the matter with you?

NONO: I don't want soup, papa.

PERELLA: Well, you'll get nothing else, soup is what we're eating.

NONO: I spy with my little eye . . .

Hesitant, mischievous, his finger coming up.
Mrs. Perella and Paolino are now in such a state of
apprehension that any movement by the captain causes
them to flinch. Mrs. Perella says in a weak, plaintive
tone:

MRS.
PERELLA: What do you spy, Nono?

PAOLINO: Bless the . . . er . . . boy.

              Nono shoves his finger out, pointing to the gâteau, the
              finger hastily withdrawn before Perella can hit it.

NONO: That!

PERELLA: What's that? A cake?

PAOLINO: Please please, my fault, I took the liberty . . .

PERELLA: You!

PAOLINO: Yes me, forgive me . . . the liberty.

PERELLA: Forgive you? What for? You brought a cake, thank you
              my dear professor.

PAOLINO: No please, it is I who must thank you.

PERELLA: Must you? For dinner? All right. We'll thank each
              other when it's finished. Done.

PAOLINO: Oh!

              A spontaneous outburst, deeply felt and instantly
              regretted.

              Let's hope so!

PERELLA: What do you mean, "let's hope so"?

PAOLINO: I mean . . . I mean when all is said and done . . . I
              mean I hope you like it, the cake.

              Nono on his knees on his chair.

NONO: I do. Great! I want some of the chocolate part.

PERELLA: Sit down! In your chair, and shut up, by God.

              Nono does with alacrity.
              Paolino is in a cold sweat, moves the cake around so
              that the chocolate part is not near to Nono, saying:

PAOLINO:	Well, well if I'd thought you were going to want the chocolate part . . . I would have brought a different part . . . cake, yes, that part isn't for you, I mean . . .
NONO:	Why not?
PAOLINO:	Not chocolate, haven't you got a headache, feverish . . . tummy trouble, didn't your mother say? Upset tummy?
NONO:	No, that's her.
PAOLINO/ MRS. PERELLA:	Nono!

Mrs. Perella's voice has changed.

NONO:	I want it! I want it!
PERELLA:	Nono! Be quiet.
PAOLINO:	I had it made specially, one half is chocolate for the grown-ups, the other half . . .
NONO:	It's chocolate I like, papa.
PERELLA:	You can have it, because I don't.
PAOLINO:	I'm appalled! I mean . . . you don't like chocolate?
PERELLA:	Not keen on it at all . . . I prefer other things . . .
PAOLINO:	My heart! My breath! Oh God . . .
PERELLA:	Appalled, heart, breath? What's up with you, professor?
PAOLINO:	Nothing, nothing . . . I hate getting things wrong. I am abject . . . sorry.
PERELLA:	Don't worry, don't take it so hard, I'll eat anything . . . anything. Anything!

He bellows.

Anything! All we're getting to eat is words. Grazia! What is she doing?

Shaking the table and shouting:

Grazia!

Enter Grazia with next course.

I want my dinner on the dot! You hear what I say? On the dot, put before me. I've told you again and again I will not wait for my food. Give it here.

He grabs for the serving dish she carries.
Food slides on the dish threatening to end up in his lap.
Perella jumps to his feet and throws the dish onto the table, breaking and scattering glasses, plates, cutlery.

Is that the way to give it to me?

GRAZIA: You snatched it! Didn't he snatch it?

PERELLA: You tipped it all over me! That's it! My appetite has gone. You may eat what's left.

Perella throwing down his napkin, about to stomp off to his room.
Stopped by a distraught Paolino.

PAOLINO: Please, captain . . .

MRS.
PERELLA: We have a guest, Francesco . . .

PERELLA: Professor, this is a madhouse. They are intent on driving me mad. Did you see?

PAOLINO: I beg you, captain, patience.

PERELLA: I swear they do it on purpose.

MRS.
PERELLA: We do all we can to please you.

PERELLA: Look at her face! Just look at it, will you?

Paolino desperately trying to placate him, lead him back to the table.

PAOLINO: I know, I know . . . but do try, for me? Like one of the family I may be, but surely I am also a guest?

PERELLA: You are, damn it, you are. All right, if you ask me to. I can't guarantee I'll be able to finish the meal but . . .

PAOLINO: Don't say that . . . surely?

PERELLA: It's been bloody years since I've been able to finish a meal in this house, it's too much!

*Nono has taken advantage of all this to kneel on his
chair and like a cat put out a paw towards the
chocolate part of the cake.*

And don't come guests with me, woman! You know
what I'm like when I'm angry, guests or no guests,
forgive me professor . . . when I see red I couldn't care
less who sits at my table, so because I'm not an animal
but a civilised human being I clear off before I do
somebody a damage . . .

*Nono swipes with his paw and licks the chocolate from
it, just like a cat, unaware that his father has seen
him.*

That! That is what I mean. Is that a well brought up
child?

*Nono is aware he is in trouble just as he is reaching out
for more licks. He freezes. Captain Perella has his ear
between finger and thumb, roaring:*

Bed! You go straight to bed without your dinner you
little pig.

*Dragged, lifted yowling from the table Nono is booted
into his room.*

I saw you, I saw you, bed!

*Exit Nono never to return. The door slammed on him.
Mrs. Perella whimpering softly, and Paolino trying to
strengthen her, though he is terrified himself.*

I can't stand it. Professor, observe, this is my life at
table. This is what happens every time I sit down to a
meal.

MRS. PERELLA:	Naughty boy, I hope, I hope . . .
PERELLA:	Eh?
MRS. PERELLA:	. . . he didn't eat much, did he?
PAOLINO:	Just a tiny scrape here.
PERELLA:	For two pins I'd toss the bloody thing into the street for the cats . . .

PAOLINO: No, you must not!

            Paolino more vehement than he intends.

PERELLA: All right, I won't . . .

PAOLINO: You wouldn't insult me like that, surely, captain?

PERELLA: No I wouldn't . . .

PAOLINO: Surely . . .

PERELLA: Let's get on with it and eat it then.

            *Paolino stunned for a second and then diving for a
            knife.*

PAOLINO: Why not? I'll cut it. Let's eat it at once! So, here we
            are, a piece for Mrs. Perella . . . This . . .

MRS.
PERELLA: Too much, too much.

PAOLINO: Dare I say, nonsense?

            *Then a thought strikes him, he looks at the cake,
            shakes his head.*

            I have to say it. It doesn't seem fair. Captain, might I
            . . . in my capacity as a teacher . . .

PERELLA: You're as soft as buggery you are. You want to give
            some to Nono don't you?

PAOLINO: Not now. No, now he is punished, quite rightly. Just
            keep him a slice, shall we? They do love cake so, it
            doesn't seem right, and I did bring it as a reward for
            his progress . . . I think all the white, don't you?

            *Perella rapping the table with his finger, delighted at
            this illustration of Paolino's soft heartedness.*

PERELLA: What did I say? Your methods are too soft, I said so,
            you couldn't be softer than that.

PAOLINO: Perhaps, perhaps . . . and this half we'll cut like this
            . . . There you are.

PERELLA: Is all that mine?

PAOLINO: I've got quite enough, thank you.

PERELLA: Come on . . . your cake, professor.

PAOLINO: I have to admit, chocolate gives me the most terrible
             heartburn . . .

PERELLA: All right . . .

             Perella wolfing his piece down.

PAOLINO: So the less I eat the better you don't know how happy
             you make me to see you tucking in with a will.

             *Immense sphincter releasing relief from Paolino and
             Mrs. Perella, they go limp as Perella eats all his cake
             making grunting noises of appreciation.*

             Happy.

MRS.
PERELLA: Oh so happy, to see you eating with such a will.
             Happy.

             Snort, grunt, wuffle from Perella.

PAOLINO: Go on, have my piece, I haven't touched it. Go on,
             please.

PERELLA: You sure?

PAOLINO: It's not good for me . . . I like it but it doesn't like me.

PERELLA: I'll have a bit of Nono's slice. He doesn't deserve all
             that . . .

PAOLINO: No, please, you know how boys like cake . . . have
             mine.

PERELLA: If it doesn't agree with you, all right.

             He eats the other piece.

             Everything agrees with me. I mean I don't really care
             for chocolate but it won't upset me. I could eat twice as
             much, three times . . .

             A belch.

             What have you got to drink?

MRS.
PERELLA: I . . . don't know.

PERELLA: Marsala, isn't there any Marsala?

MRS.
PERELLA: I don't . . .

PERELLA: Nice drop of Marsala, go down very well . . .

MRS.
PERELLA: . . . think we've got any.

PERELLA: Last straw! She invites you to dinner and no bloody
             Marsala. What do you think of that?

             Perella building himself up into a rage again.

PAOLINO: Well, as for me . . .

PERELLA: I know that. But what about the principle of the thing?
             What sort of a wife is it doesn't remember the Marsala?
             There's no effort put into it. No foresight, no planning,
             no housekeeping . . . what? Too busy tarting herself
             up. Aren't you?

MRS.
PERELLA: It's the first time, Francesco.

PERELLA: I see you don't deny it.

MRS.
PERELLA: No, but . . .

             *Perella gets to his feet, tugs at the tablecloth and
             scatters everything from the table.*

PERELLA: Answer me back would you, by God!

MRS.
PERELLA: What did I say?

PERELLA: You said "but", you said "the first time", and my girl
             it had better be the last time. I know what your game
             is. But you won't catch me. I'm too bloody clever for
             you. I'd rather jump out of the window any jumping to
             be done! Go fuck yourself!

             Exit Perella. The bolt on his door.
             Silence.
             Dusk.
             A great sadness descends.
             The two lovers look at each other across the table,
             exhausted, swaying slightly with faintness.
             The light fading.

Enter Grazia.
She raises her hands in the air once, walks forward
slowly, her feet placed carefully, raises her hands
again, twice, another walk, and then her hands up
finally to say:

GRAZIA: As usual.

MRS.
PERELLA: Oh yes, as usual.

A totally normal voice.

Go to bed, Grazia, when you wish, this can be left
until morning. Don't make a noise, he will hear.

GRAZIA: Shall I put a light on?

MRS.
PERELLA: Oh no, thank you, we don't want light.

GRAZIA: As usual. The same ruction every time, every single
time . . . what a mess!

Exit Grazia.

What a to-doment . . . !

Paolino and Mrs. Perella totally dejected.
Through the open window on the verandah can be
heard the sea.
Moonlight. A beam of moonlight becomes brighter and
illuminates the five pot plants between the two doors.

MRS.
PERELLA: He would rather throw himself out of the window.

PAOLINO: There's time. We must wait, that's all . . . wait!

MRS.
PERELLA: What do we wait for?

PAOLINO: I am assured it will work, they both said so, the
brothers, one a doctor the other a pharmacist, they
must be right.

MRS.
PERELLA: They don't know him. Nor do you, Paolino. He would
rather jump from the window.

PAOLINO: You mustn't give in. If you think that, if you're going to admit defeat . . .

MRS.
PERELLA: I'm here, I'll sit here all night long.

PAOLINO: Won't do if you don't have confidence.

MRS.
PERELLA: It's no good. I know.

PAOLINO: *Will* him to come to you. Be confident he will. There is a great deal to be said for the power of the mind. I'm sure of it. It is our only hope. Think of him, try to attract him with your thoughts, mind power. You must be confident, you must know that he will come to you, you must . . . otherwise we are done for, doomed, the abyss yawns and it will swallow us, true. I am in dread of what I might do tomorrow if you fail. I do beg you, my love, my heart . . .

MRS.
PERELLA: Then here I shall sit.

> *A large antique chair. She sits on it outside her husband's room.*
> *Music.*
> *The hush of a church.*
> *Moonlight on her as she sits so that should her husband come out he will find her.*

PAOLINO: Yes, like that, what . . . what . . . behold the handmaiden of the Lord, behold she is washed in moonlight, good, oh my saint! A sign, show me a sign tomorrow at dawn. I shall not sleep . . . I'll be round here at dawn to see . . . er . . . to know. A sign. One of those pot plants on the verandah, if all is well, if it's yes. Yes. Where I can see it from the street, first light, dawn tomorrow. Can I ask you to do that? You do look like a saint, so . . . until tomorrow.

> *Paolino backing away in something like awe, almost as if he hears the music breathing into the room.*

MRS.
PERELLA: Until tomorrow, Paolino.

He is at the door now, their voices whispers.
He joins his hands together in prayer.

PAOLINO: Let it be thus.

MRS.
PERELLA: Behold the handmaiden of the Lord: be it done to me
             according to thy word.

             Exit Paolino.

             And the angel departed from her.

ACT THREE

The sound of seagulls and fishing boats.

Scene: House of Captain Perella, in Leghorn 1919.

> *Dawn's early light.*
> *The morning after. There are no pot plants on the verandah.*
> *The room is as it was the night before, some of it cleared by the grumbling Grazia, but not much.*
>
> *Enter Grazia.*
>
> *She gets down on her knees at the table and starts to pick up glasses, broken bits of crockery.*
> *Whenever she straightens she fumes and shakes a fist at the door of the room occupied by Captain Perella.*
> *It's her kidneys. They're agony.*

GRAZIA: He's a pig, in a palace, which he's turning into a pig-sty. Do you hear me? You're turning it into a pig sty for yourself, don't think I don't know. My word! A bottle in one piece. You missed this one, you pig! Ooooooooooh! My kidneys kill me. They do. This is the house of a pig! Why I bother I don't know, he'll come out of there and snuffle and snort and bash.

> *A bell rings.*

That's the front door. Who is at the front door? Nobody should be. Oooooooooooooooh, my God!

> *Getting up to go to the door and gesturing towards the door of the room occupied by the Captain.*

You have ruined my kidneys, you pig.

> *Exit Grazia.*
> *Re-enter Grazia with Filippo the sailor.*

I can't see anything, can you? Where does she usually have it put?

FILIPPO: At the door. Is he not sailing?

GRAZIA: Sleeping as far as I know, not sailing.

FILIPPO: I want his sea-going gear. She should have put it up last night.

GRAZIA: I know she should, but she didn't.

FILIPPO: Why didn't she?

GRAZIA: She had other things to think about.

FILIPPO: I can see the mess.

GRAZIA: Oh yes.

FILIPPO: He went spare didn't he?

GRAZIA: He played the very devil.

FILIPPO: That's what I mean, smashed the lot as per . . .

GRAZIA: That's nothing.

FILIPPO: Is that right?

Filippo waits, agog. Grazia says nothing but nods her head a lot.

What did he do?

GRAZIA: What didn't he do?

FILIPPO: Yes?

GRAZIA: Well . . .

FILIPPO: Go on . . . ? Have a go at the wife, knock her about did he? That right? Terrible. I'm not surprised. What about the boy, belt him did he? Terrible. That right? You? Give you a belting did he? Oh my word!

Grazia is about to answer him and then thinks better of it.

GRAZIA: I have work to do.

FILIPPO: So he did, did he?

GRAZIA: Let me get on.

FILIPPO: You should see him in Naples, meek as a lamb.

GRAZIA: Lamb! He's a swine.

FILIPPO: Yes, he's a swine as well. He's a swine here and a lamb in Naples.

GRAZIA: What's she like, young?

FILIPPO: That's right, young, she gives it him.

GRAZIA: Does she?

FILIPPO: Never seen anything like it, built like a dreadnaught
            she is, arms on her like a stevedore, she gives it him all
            right, tits like . . . a ten-inch gun turret, thighs like
            anchor cables. I've been going to that house he keeps
            for her in Naples ever since I shipped under him.
            Fetch his gear, that sort of thing. I've seen her give
            him a backhander lifted him clean across the room
            faster than a typhoon tidies loose dunnage. Ugly as sin
            she is, face like a ship's biscuit, but he seems to love
            her, she seems to keep him busy, drops a kid a year,
            that's what's ruining him of course, how many is it
            now, six? That's right, six. I suppose he gets what he
            wants, never mind the bruises.

GRAZIA: Not enough though is it?

FILIPPO: Who for? Her . . . ?

GRAZIA: No, him. Some men can't get enough of anything.

FILIPPO: Oh you mean here, his wife here.

GRAZIA: Wife! He doesn't give her the time of day. Wife
            indeed!

FILIPPO: He hasn't been giving it you, has he?

GRAZIA: What!

FILIPPO: The time of day.

GRAZIA: You mind your own business.

FILIPPO: Randy old bugger.

GRAZIA: What?

FILIPPO: Captain of the lugger.

GRAZIA: Yes, well.

FILIPPO: That's right, that's right . . .

            *Filippo contemplating Grazia in a new light, then
            roars with laughter.*

... very true. Anything.

GRAZIA: Are you going?

FILIPPO: I am my dear, yes, but I'll come back later see you're all right ... tell his missus I called for his nibs' dunnage will you? See you later then ... er ... Grazia, see you're all right. My word.

Exit Filippo.

GRAZIA: Hhhhmmmmmm!

Grazia on the floor looking for unbroken pieces still, under the table cloth, straightening up and complaining about her kidneys as she does so, putting things back on the table.
The sound of the bolt being drawn in the room occupied by the Captain.
Enter Captain Perella.
Still sleepy, dark shadows under his eyes, in a foul temper.

Here comes the wild pig from his sty!

PERELLA: What did you say? Who were you talking to. I heard you yammering on ...

GRAZIA: Your cabin boy.

PERELLA: You watch your language, what did he want?

GRAZIA: Your stuff.

PERELLA: How about a good morning?

GRAZIA: This is my good morning ... clearing up after you.

PERELLA: What were you doing last night?

Grazia looks up at him, a long hard insolent stare, then she goes back to her work.
Perella looms over her, demands:

Come on! What were you doing last night that you couldn't clear up then?

GRAZIA: What was I doing?

She sits on her heels and looks at him again.

Well you might ask. You come off that ship, you lash

out at everyone and everything, you wreak havoc with the dishes and the food and the furniture and the carpet, you compel people to do things . . . provide services they are not obliged to . . .

PERELLA: Coffee!

GRAZIA: Not ready.

PERELLA: I'll give you not ready . . .

> *Perella draws back his hand to strike her, she scuttles away from him.*

GRAZIA: You lay a finger on me and I'll yell blue murder!

PERELLA: Make me some coffee at once! Everybody knows I want coffee, ready, soon as I turn out.

GRAZIA: I'm amazed you can lift your head, after what you got up to last night, crack of dawn . . . !

PERELLA: Enough of your lip!

GRAZIA: What is it? No rest for the wicked?

PERELLA: Coffeeeeee! Woman!

GRAZIA: That's what it is . . .

> *Exit Grazia.*
> *Perella left in the midst of the debris, growling, yawning, snorting:*

PERELLA: I don't know what gets into people.

> *His brows furrow. He thinks, feet pawing the ground, while he does so, eyes darting.*
> *Then he yawns again and gnashes his teeth, shakes his head, pads about the room, stops and expels air.*
> *Like a dog he pants with the heat, pulling at his clothes, his tongue out, going to the verandah for air.*
> *He's hot! It's stifling!*
> *He shuffles, stands on the verandah looking at the sea and moans almost piteously:*

The sea . . .

> *Sniffing for the smell of the sea, then taking in a great shuddering breath.*
> *Hands on the balcony rails, head up and down again,*

*as if he is contemplating a dive, a flight into the waters
of the sea his home.*
*On one of his glances down he sees Paolino looking up
at him and releases a great sigh of:*

Good morning professor, you look up at me, you do
. . . what do you do this hour, very first light? What?
Do you? So do I, indeed, a breath of sea air, this
delightful breeze . . . isn't it? Come up, come up, have
some coffee . . . why don't you?

*Watching Paolino walk round to the entrance to the
house and waiting, looking into the room, gently
snuffling.*
*Enter Paolino with the lack of co-ordination of a
madman, arms, legs everywhere, face chalk white, eyes
determined on murder.*

Quick as a flash. Did you run?

PAOLINO: You saw me, you saw me did you? On my way back
from the harbour.

PERELLA: I saw your white face, nose tilted up, tucked into the
shadows below my balcony.

PAOLINO: Yes yes, of course but I had been to the harbour you
see and on the way back I was going past and there was
this group of people shouting and making a commotion
. . . Ah, thought I, something has fallen from the
balcony, something like a pot plant, that sort of thing.
Has one?

PERELLA: Has one?

PAOLINO: Yes, placed in the window.

PERELLA: No, not as far as I know.

PAOLINO: I could have sworn . . .

PERELLA: I know nothing of pot plants.

PAOLINO: I saw some broken pieces of plant pot on the ground I
thought in the knot of people making this commotion
under your balcony when I was on my way up from
. . . so I thought aaaah, I know what all this fuss is
about . . .

PERELLA: I heard no commotion.

PAOLINO: You sure? You certain there wasn't a pot plant on the balcony?

PERELLA: All the pot plants are over there.

PAOLINO: Good good, how many? Five . . .

PERELLA: Five.

PAOLINO: Always been five? Yes.

PERELLA: Yes, no room for any more, professor.

PAOLINO: Five. In which case . . . yes . . . nothing at all.

PERELLA: Don't look so disappointed, I'll throw one out for you.

PAOLINO: Please no . . . ha ha . . . no, it's just that with all the . . . coming back . . . You know how it is.

> *Paolino pulling himself together, and talking to the captain about imagination even though half way through he realises that the captain only dimly understands the concept.*

You know. Imagination, how it works. Why. I mean how sometimes your imagination runs away with you, all sorts of things enter your mind, you even begin to think that what you see is real, I was certain when I saw the commotion under the . . . as I went by . . . there must have been a pot plant, that's what they're on about and it must have . . .

PERELLA: Funny I heard nothing in the street.

PAOLINO: That's all right then . . . let's forget it! It's forgotten.

> *Paolino peers at the dense mass of hair and terror that is the captain's face, asks:*

I hope you don't mind me saying . . . ?

PERELLA: What?

PAOLINO: Nothing . . .

> *Paolino looking intently at the captain's face. Perella puzzled, bristling.*

PERELLA: Eh?

PAOLINO: You look awfully . . . you look . . .

PERELLA: How do I look?

PAOLINO: As if you got up very early.

PERELLA: Looks as if you did too.

PAOLINO: Yes?

> *Both men with their faces very close together, as if they might each go for the throat of the other. Each looking at the other very closely, suspiciously:*

PERELLA: Down the harbour and back up again.

PAOLINO: Yes, yes . . .

PERELLA: You're odd this morning.

PAOLINO: A bit . . . tense.

PERELLA: Walk in the fresh air. Does you good.

PAOLINO: It does do, yes.

> *They break. Captain Perella amused perhaps, turning his back and going to the balcony.*
> *Paolino crumpling and uttering in a strangled voice:*

I will kill him. My word of honour I'll do it!

PERELLA: Nothing better when you're strung. Good blow. All your daft notions go . . .

PAOLINO: Oh you are so right, I slept badly last night. Not a wink . . .

PERELLA: Me too. Damn it!

PAOLINO: You too? Ah . . . ah . . .

> *Brightening, anxious.*

. . . and?

PERELLA: What?

PAOLINO: I couldn't help noticing, shadows under your eyes, you must have had a rotten night . . . a wearing night . . . ?

PERELLA: I never closed my eyes. A pig of a night. Too bloody hot, sweating buckets . . .

PAOLINO: Oh it was, a sweltering night . . .

PERELLA: Stifling!

PAOLINO: Which is why you . . . got out of bed I suppose,
          perhaps . . . you would, I did, I did.

PERELLA: Did I?

          Captain Perella glares at him.

PAOLINO: I expect so. When your bed is so hot, what else? The
          heat and all . . . your room must have been like an
          oven . . . mine was.

PERELLA: An oven, you're right.

PAOLINO: I expect you came out?

          *Perella looks at Paolino for a moment then says
          darkly:*

PERELLA: I did. I was suffocating.

          Enter Grazia with coffee on a salver.

          Coffee. About time. Only one cup? What's he going to
          drink out of?

GRAZIA: You didn't tell me about him.

PERELLA: Don't talk to me like that. Do I have to tell you
          everything? That woman takes too many liberties.

GRAZIA: Liberties!

          She spits with scorn.

          Liberties indeed.

PERELLA: Yes, too many liberties!

GRAZIA: Makes a change.

PERELLA: What do you mean?

GRAZIA: I'm the one taking liberties now am I?

PERELLA: Bloody cheek. You'll be out on your ear!

GRAZIA: Is that so? I know one or two things about you I could
          tell. You won't sack me for fear I'll tell somebody what
          you've been up to . . .

PERELLA: Eh?

             *Paolino has been listening and watching with slowly
             dawning suspicion.*
             *He sways slightly, moans gently: Oh God, Oh
             God . . .*

             Professor, you hear the slut?

PAOLINO: Oh I do . . . I do . . .

             Perella growls at Grazia.

PERELLA: I've had just about enough from you, woman . . .

GRAZIA: Not half of what I've had . . .

PERELLA: Go and get another cup of coffee for the professor. At
             once! Here, you, have this one.

             Giving Paolino his cup.

PAOLINO: No thank you . . .

             To Grazia.

             . . . please don't trouble.

PERELLA: Take it.

PAOLINO: No.

PERELLA: Yes.

PAOLINO: Not good for me.

PERELLA: Not good for you . . . go and get him a cup.

PAOLINO: No no thank you, I'm too . . . too . . . already.

             *Grazia looking from one to the other, hand on hip,
             insolent.*
             *Paolino shakes his head at her, he can't believe she's
             the same woman.*
             He finishes lamely:

             Jumpy, on edge . . . coffee would make it worse.

GRAZIA: Are you sure? Well . . . ? Yes? No?

PERELLA: Clear off!

             Exit Grazia and Perella shouts after her:

I can see you're going to need another lesson in manners, woman. Mend your manners or I'll give you one.

PAOLINO: She does take an amazing amount of liberties for a mere servant.

PERELLA: Keep them too long, they do.

PAOLINO: I know nothing about that. I would think that they should know their place, know who's boss, no matter what they're asked to do.

PERELLA: What are you getting at, professor?

PAOLINO: I am simply saying that I am amazed, astounded . . .

PERELLA: At that woman's arrogance?

PAOLINO: Yes, but more than that . . . that you well, that you . . .

PERELLA: What?

PAOLINO: Put up with it. How has this come to pass, what is going on, am I to believe that you and she . . . er? Is it possible?

PERELLA: Yes, it is shocking.

PAOLINO: Shocking!

PERELLA: It's my wife's fault.

PAOLINO: Oh come now, you can hardly blame your wife!

PERELLA: She keeps her on. Not me. Sentiment. She saw Nono born. She knows our ways . . . that sort of drivel. She's used to us.

Paolino heatedly, indignantly:

PAOLINO: Is that any reason for you to behave towards her . . . the way you do?

PERELLA: Don't take the high horse with me!

PAOLINO: I'm sorry. I just think it's going too far to blame your wife.

PERELLA: I blame everyone. This house drives me mad. I hate it, I curse it from the moment I set foot in it . . . it suffocates me. I expect it's the heat. I can never sleep. And when I can't sleep I get angry.

PAOLINO: Whose fault is that? Who can you blame for the weather?

PERELLA: Me! I'll blame me, I don't mind blaming me, I'm angry with the bloody weather, I'm angry with the bloody house . . . because I need air. Wind. Sea. I'm used to being at sea. To tell the truth I cannot stand being ashore, dear professor, you'll understand, makes me angry do you see . . . especially when it's hot, when it's summer, bloody walls you see, can't abide them . . . walls, windows, women.

PAOLINO: Even women?

PERELLA: Like walls, they get in the way. Yes, most of all women. As far as women are concerned, what are we talking about, I'm a sailor . . . got one in every port, well not these days perhaps, getting on now, more interested in comfort now, but I haven't gone short, still don't. But tell you one thing, I'm not a slave to it, know what I mean, whiff of stinky finger and at it like a dog? Not me, that's the good thing about me, when I want it I have it, when I don't, fuck it . . .

             He roars with laughter.

             I'm the captain of any ship I'm on.

PAOLINO: Is that . . . true?

PERELLA: Fact. Only when I feel like it. What about you? Doesn't take much to get you going, does it?

PAOLINO: I would rather not be brought into this, please.

PERELLA: What does she have to do? Little smile . . . eh? Slipping eyes . . . eh?

             Paolino is uncomfortable and furious.

             Up it comes, eh? Whoops pardon me miss, got to sit down somewhere, pardon me . . .

PAOLINO: Please . . .

PERELLA: Bit shy are you? Hold hands do you?

PAOLINO: For heaven's sake captain, I'm not in the mood for this.

PERELLA: Got to be love with you I expect. Full of poetry I
             expect, and scruples, I expect you go a bundle on
             scruples . . . tell me? Tell me the truth, teacher?

             Paolino snaps.

PAOLINO: I'll tell you one thing, if I had a wife . . .

             Perella roars with laughter.

             Don't laugh at me you . . . don't laugh!

PERELLA: Wives! Where do wives come into it? I'm talking about
             women.

PAOLINO: Wives are women.

PERELLA: Wives can be . . . sometimes.

             *The two men are now face to face shouting at each
             other. No laughter now.*

PAOLINO: You admit it then!

PERELLA: Sometimes.

PAOLINO: Fine.

PERELLA: Fine?

PAOLINO: Sometimes a husband must look on his wife as a
             woman.

PERELLA: That's what I said.

PAOLINO: Fine.

PERELLA: You can be sure a wife will show she's a woman to
             some other bloke if he doesn't.

PAOLINO: If he forgets she's a woman.

PERELLA: That's right. I said that.

PAOLINO: So if he's got any sense he doesn't forget that?

PERELLA: That's right, I said that. He'll make sure . . .

             Perella calms, laughs, says ruefully:

             You haven't got a wife though, professor, and I hope
             for your own good you never do have.

*Paolino not wanting to change mood, still irritable,
trying to provoke the captain and himself into a real
fight, winding up his own courage.*

PAOLINO: That's not what you just said.

PERELLA: About what?

PAOLINO: About me.

PERELLA: You?

PAOLINO: Yes me . . . me!

PERELLA: What did I say?

PAOLINO: You said I was an ideal . . . you said I was full of
scruples and love . . .

PERELLA: You want to get married do you?

PAOLINO: Do I? I didn't say that.

PERELLA: Sounds like it to me.

PAOLINO: I'm talking about me. You've got the wrong idea about
me altogether.

PERELLA: Is that right?

PAOLINO: Yes.

PERELLA: I'm wrong about you.

PAOLINO: Yes. And . . . and you're wrong about other things as
well, you're terribly wrong, you're committing a grave
injustice.

PERELLA: To you?

PAOLINO: To me, yes, and to wives.

PERELLA: Wives?

PAOLINO: Definitely.

PERELLA: You what? You standing up for wives are you? You
know why, don't you? Because you haven't got one.
You know why, don't you, because you don't need one.
I expect you use other people's!

Paolino screams at the captain:

PAOLINO: How dare you say that to me!

Perella dismayed at his violent reaction.

PERELLA: Professor . . .

PAOLINO: Don't professor me, how dare you say that to my face!
                You insult me deeply. As you would any honest man. I
                am a man of conscience, I have principles and scruples,
                yes scruples. I have! I am! I find myself through no
                fault of my own, without intention, in a very awkward
                situation but, it is not true that I make use of the wives
                of other men, not true at all, how dare you say it! Were
                I such a person, did I behave in such a way would I be
                likely to insist that no husband should neglect his wife?
                I did say that, you can't deny it, and I meant it with
                all my heart and soul. Is this the sentiment of a man
                intent on debauching other men's wives? I'll go further.
                Yes. Any man who neglects his wife is guilty of a
                criminal act, acts! Not merely against the wife, most
                likely a perfectly virtuous woman compelled by force of
                circumstance to fail in her duty but also against the
                man, compelled to be unhappy for ever, all his life, for
                ever and ever!

                    *Paolino casting about on the table for something,
                    anything, a weapon of some kind, finding and casting
                    aside spoons, napkins, pieces of crockery, all useless.*

                Driven to thoughts of . . . yes, who knows? Compelled
                by sharing in the suffering of this poor woman, this
                wretched man will be brought to the edge . . .

                    A fork found, gripped.

                So much so that he will even contemplate the loss of
                his liberty, his life . . . oh yes, an honest man driven to
                violent extremes. I tell you and I mean it, captain . . .

                    Alarm, shock.

MRS.
PERELLA: What on earth is going on?

                    *Enter Mrs. Perella, dishevelled, her face puffed and
                    smeared, exhausted, her voice weak and husky.
                    Paolino drops the fork.
                    Perella explains:*

PERELLA: I don't know what's got into him. Ranting on about wives and husbands and suffering.

PAOLINO: I said . . .

MRS.
PERELLA: Ssssssshhhhhhh, stop it, please.

Mrs. Perella could do with a good night's sleep. She yawns.
Languorously. Then says to Paolino:

Help me with these pot plants, professor.

Paolino beams in relief.

PAOLINO: Oh . . . yes.

Grabs a pot plant.

This one? On the verandah? Where . . . ?

MRS.
PERELLA: Yes, but give me that one. You bring another, if you don't mind.

Mrs. Perella trailing to the verandah with the pot plant.

PAOLINO: Mind? I'm delighted!

Following her to the verandah.

Where shall I put it? Here?

MRS.
PERELLA: Yes thank you.

Mrs. Perella goes back to collect a third and fourth pot plant.
Paolino is overjoyed. He embraces the astonished Captain Perella.

PAOLINO: Forgive me, captain. What must you have taken me for? What must you have thought?

PERELLA: Eh?

PAOLINO: I was on edge, up early, down to the harbour but still . . . on edge, I must thank you for letting me go on, listening to me so patiently, it's always the way with me, if I can only get rid of some of my pent up emotions I feel so much better . . . As I do now! I do thank you, captain, from the bottom of my heart. What a lovely day it is. Look at that sky! And look at those . . . five?

Mrs. Perella holding the last pot plant, a magnificent lily, she modest, eyes lowered.

Plants are so . . . they . . . these five pot plants . . . they . . .

MRS.
PERELLA: Give new life?

PAOLINO: . . . to a house, yes, they do. I have to say it, captain, I do thank you, and you must forgive me . . . I have been a beast!

Perella nods, shakes his head sententiously:

PERELLA: Professor, we must be men! We must be men, not beasts.

PAOLINO: So we must, we must. It's easy for you, captain, with a wife like you have, virtue personified.

Curtain.

FURTHER PLAYS AVAILABLE FROM ABSOLUTE CLASSICS

PAINS OF YOUTH
Ferdinand Bruckner
Translated by Daphne Moore

'Discovery of the Year'
GUARDIAN

£4.50

A FAMILY AFFAIR
Alexander Ostrovsky
Adapted by Nick Dear

'a stinging and scurrilously funny version by Nick Dear'
OBSERVER

£4.50

THUNDER IN THE AIR
August Strindberg
Translated by Eivor Martinus

'a sulphurous, atmospheric work full of summer lightning'
GUARDIAN

£4.50

TURCARET
Alain-René Lesage
Translated/adapted by John Norman

'One of the best of French comedies'
SUNDAY TELEGRAPH

£4.50

THE POWER OF DARKNESS
Leo Tolstoy
Translated/adapted by Anthony Clark

'THE POWER OF DARKNESS rends the air with greatness'
SPECTATOR

£4.50

ANATOL

Arthur Schnitzler

Translated by Michael Robinson

'Schnitzler's most amusing and original play'

DAILY TELEGRAPH

£4.50

THERESE RAQUIN

Emile Zola

Translated by Pip Broughton

'A gripping yarn'

GUARDIAN

£3.95

COLLECTIONS

FALSE ADMISSIONS, SUCCESSFUL STRATEGIES, LA DISPUTE

Marivaux

Translated by Timberlake Wertenbaker

'the most succe ful English translator of Marivaux in the present age, if not ever'

OBSERVER

£5.50

FUENTE OVEJUNA, LOST IN A MIRROR

Lope de Vega

Adapted by Adrian Mitchell

'It is hard to imagine a more gripping tale than the one which emerges in Adrian Mitchell's translation'

TIME OUT

£5.95

THE LIAR, THE ILLUSION

Pierre Corneille

Translated/adapted by Ranjit Bolt

Two contrasting plays from one of France's major classic playwrights in an elegant new translation.

£5.50

DUE